A Lifetime of Conversion

By

Richard D. Green

A LIFETIME OF CONVERSION

by Richard D. Green

Threshold Publishing
SLC, UT 84171

Cover layout - Richard D. Green
Cover Art Work - William A. (Bill) Green

For inquiries contact: thresholdpublishing@yahoo.com

Available on Amazon
ISBN-13: 978-0-9915163-0-77

List Price $12.99

Prayer & Patience

All of our searches in this life for God and the individual path He has set before us should turn us to prayer. Prayer is one of our greatest blessings and the most effective tool at our disposal. Without prayer we are left to resolve things by ourselves in darkness, confusion and fear.

Patience is to wait for the things you pray for; waiting for them to happen when you are worthy or for them to happen in God's timeframe. Patience is to allow the Lord to give you experiences and knowledge so you are able to receive those answers you pray for and better understand them.

A prayer offered in faith establishes the expectation that some form of an answer may be received. However, without a history of receiving answers from God, often subtle, silent messages from the Spirit are unknowingly received. Through frequent reflection of your inquiries of God, you may begin to find a pattern, through which, God has left somewhat obscure answers. Using someone else's template of how God communicates with the human family is as erroneous as believing everyone's relationship with God is the same.

I have had many spiritual experiences throughout the years and have always thought of them as unique and separate. I did not see any correlation between them; yet one day as I pondered them as a whole, I realized they were all tied to prayer. There might have been unique lessons or gospel principles associated with each; however they all involved prayer. I realized all those things were tied to God or gave me one more token toward arriving at His doorstep. So why would they not be laced with prayer; the means we have to directly communicate with God?

The following chapters are pages from my life. By sharing these very personal experiences, I hope it will illustrate how God established a pattern of how He communicates with me. Sometimes it has been less than subtle and other times quite obscure. The pattern is not so much, how He communicates with me; but more, how I am required to provide an effort in seeking His answers. However, I also feel when more fully living according to the covenants I have made with God the answers seem to come easier and more frequently.

Seeing a daily increase of decay in the world in which we live, I find myself more often seeking guidance and answers through prayer. I also pay closer attention to the words of modern day prophets, as God has always used His prophets to warn and prepare the world against Satan's evil deceptions. For years, those prophets have told us we are living in the Last Days. But in the immediate past, they have boldly declared that we are in the last of the Last Days. During this year President Nelson openly warned that time is running out.

This is the time that scripture tells us: even the elite will be deceived. It is also a time that utilization of prayer should be at an all time high. However, the scriptures indicate that pride will be at an all time high rather than prayer, during these last days.

Casual observations of the world around, clearly testify that the prophesied indicators above are happening before our very eyes. Painfully, I have recently watched strong, long time members of the LDS church criticize church leader, even prophets. Many have left the church due to statements or actions of others. A world that is thriving on contention has wrapped its arms around even the elite, pulling them into a battle, where there is no representation from the Holy Spirit of peace. And in all this dramatic deviation from long term practices and beliefs, there is hardly a prayer offered in seeking direction. Instead, the ballooning pride of man offers suggestions and remedies that are far from what a humbled heart would find, when seeking divine guidance through prayer.

I hope the following pages will aid others in avoiding deception, such as the master of deceit inflicted upon me; who successfully stalled my spiritual growth, through pride and a fear of prayer.

Table of Contents

Chapter 1.

A LIFETIME OF CONVERSION

From a very early age I was introduced to "good versus evil". Not the element pertaining to imaginary characters, but two opposing forces that I found to be very real and tangible. Even as I began grade school, there seemed to be a battle of competing influences that I was aware of.

As my eighth birthday approached, my excitement grew, it being the date I would be baptized into the Church of Jesus Christ. I accepted the belief that when I was baptized, I would be cleansed of all my sins. I also believed anything I did from then on would leave its mark upon me; not understanding the concept of repentance and the atonement of Jesus Christ. After being baptized on Saturday; I wondered if anyone noticed the glow that surely surrounded me as I stepped off the school bus on Monday morning. Exiting the building at morning recess, I sprinted through the cold winter air to occupy one of the four squares painted on the playground. Within minutes someone slide a spinning serve across the edge of my square; the ball just beyond my reach. Instantly a few commonly linked words rolled off my tongue, just as easily as they had the week before. At the end of the game I walked away a little weighted down. There was a slight sense of embarrassment; oh, I hoped no one had heard what had come out of my mouth. But more than that was the disappointment that the armor, I was supposed to have received the previous weekend, didn't really aid me in the least. In fact, I noticed during the next few days the number of infractions dropping weight upon my shoulders was hitting an all time high. "Or was it just because I was more aware of it now", a suggestion offered to my mind.

Like all the rowdy young boys around me, my language got more colorful each year. Then progression took hold within my little band of brothers. Stealing from Evil Knievel's aging aunt and uncle's little store, across the street from our grade school, became a badge of belonging. But when I would get home and sit alone in my bedroom, I wondered if any of them felt the growing guilt and shame that had replaced the glow I had felt for such a short time. Most of them went to church, just like I did, but they didn't seem to have the conflict that plagued me.

New class, new school, it didn't matter; it was as if the same type of friends were there, waiting my arrival. How did I always find those select few that loved mischief as much as I did; pushing the envelope on everything placed before us? It made for a very exciting childhood; however, the humor got harder to find as we moved though the years. Today, it stirs emotion whenever I look back and recall the carnage that came upon so many of the dear friends of my youth. I have watched many suffer from alcohol or drug addiction, broken marriages, jail or prison time, an early death or so many other agents of sorrow. My mind tires as I try to determine why so few of us were able to travel through that unseen battleground, to later find the joys of a life blessed with families, success and longevity. I find no commonality that would determine which group any of us would have been assigned to. Each group had those that came from good homes, broken homes, church going or alcoholic environments, small and large families.

I can only speak with authority on what molded my values, shaping the events throughout my life; which, ultimately provided me with a better than deserved outcome. I can promise I didn't get to this place in my life unscathed. Nor do I expect the future to be without more of the same uphill battle. But in striving each day to become more like my Savior, I have found myself standing in an amazing calm; which, is full of contentment and hope.

The following pages are filled with scenes from my life. They are not intended to give anyone a road map to success or happiness. Every person has a unique path to follow. Like myself, you may look back at points on your own path and claim you were left with no choice; as if destiny blocked all routes but one. Yet, so many times the correct choices seemed obscure; determining years later any choice may have gotten you to where you ended up. Those two repeating scenarios have led me to believe God has a personal plan designed just for me. Choices I make or that others make, may impact God's plan. However, His plan will not be frustrated; as He will provide altered plans to provide those things that I remain worthy to receive. I share the very personal experiences of my life in hopes that it may lead others to find their unique pattern that God uses to communicate with them. The examples throughout scripture that give hints as to how God communicated with people, may be hard to find and often hard to decipher. By seeing the extreme patience God exercised as he molded and directed me to where I stand today; my prayer is that it may help others find their own conduit to God.

Without taking the time for deep reflective understanding, my life may have felt like a bunch of hurdles with some joy and success mixed in. But as time has passed, when able to push self pity aside, each challenge has become a sweet memory, embedding a sense of victory and accomplishment. C.S. Lewis so perfectly described how we may view life at its conclusion. He indicated that for the good man, even the bitter challenges of life will become sweet memories, feeling he was always in heaven. Yet for the bad man, all the evil committed for pleasure will become a bitter memory, feeling he was always in hell.

Some may read this and determine I have no ability to speak of a challenged life, as they may have experienced tragedy I can't even begin to fathom. Others may not be able to relate, having experienced life as more of a pleasure cruise. I assume;

3

however, that we have all experienced our own sorrow or demons that have left lasting scars.

I am not delusional enough to profess that I can provide a step by step program; enabling others to find their joy in the midst of a very complex world. However, I sincerely hope exposing my hidden secrets and joys will create a desire in others to examine their rearward path. Pondering one's past as a massive, well orchestrated plan, may bring to light the purpose for many of the struggles and accomplishments that seemed so senseless and without purpose at the time. By understanding one's past, the offered direction of their future may become more evident. Through prayerful pleas, they may begin to recognize a lighted pathway; which will lead them to their desired destination.

Chapter 2.

UNCERTAINTY

As a child, I did the normal routine of stealing from the corner grocery store, more humorous than it was serious. And I participated in all those pranks that bordered on vandalism. Those however, are not the types of things that are too detrimental to someone's future. But as I emerged from childhood, it was as if I had a determination to see how close I could push all the boundaries and still not cross into eternal damnation.

In the seventh grade, I was quite short and wrestled in the 76 pound weight class. The only parts of my body that had experienced a growth spurt were my ears and cheeks. I am still amazed a person can be so skinny and yet look so large from the neck up. I was very nice to girls; because, most of them had already had a growth spurt by that age and towered over me. That is a painful point of creation I fully believe God put in place just to give adults an occasional smile. My small stature had developed a rather quick wit and sharp tongue. I believe that may have been a contributing factor to the reason a 200 pound eighth-grader was chasing me through the halls one afternoon. Just before he caught me, I recalled putting a switch blade knife in my pocket that morning. I put it there to be cool at recess; however, pulling it out was an act of desperation. I would never have believed I would pull a knife on someone, yet a scenario suddenly developed that provoked a decision that often changes lives forever. He must have sensed my immense fear, as he swore at me and then just walked off. Why he didn't tell a teacher or do something further, I will never know. I do know that after he left, I started shaking and nearly threw up thinking about what almost took place. That day I threw the knife in the garbage and decided it would be better to take a punch, than to stab someone.

I began drinking in the eighth grade and smoking marijuana by the ninth grade. When I was a junior in high school I took a shot at growing some marijuana plants. After a few weeks the plants were getting too big to keep from being detected. My friend and I decided to move them to his house on Sunday afternoon, while my family was in church. I only lived a block from the church, so it was pretty easy to determine when the coast was clear. As we drove past the church I felt some relief knowing the plants were out of my house. After making a left turn I immediately saw flashing lights in my mirror as adrenaline began pumping through my body. I could only assume the policeman that was pulling me over had no idea I was transporting marijuana and had his lights on for some other reason. As I calmly walked back toward his car with my driver's license in hand, he began approaching me. Never in my life have I felt so invisible. He proceeded right to the passenger door of my car. It turned out that as I was walking back to his car, he saw my friend attempt to cover the plants that were between his feet. The officer's comment was something about us trying to put the greenhouse out of business.

We waited quite some time for the wrecker to arrive. As I looked across the field at the church, one can't imagine the regret I felt of not being in attendance that day. My anxiety grew as it neared time for church to get out. What an impression I would have made on all the members if they were to drive by before we were gone. Luckily the officer became impatient and decided to take us to the police station. I was arrested for manufacturing a controlled substance; which amounted to a felony in those days.

After what seemed to be an eternity, my mother arrived and they brought her into the room. The officer began to explain that I was being released into her custody. When she asked, "Why!" he began to explain the principles of releasing a minor into the custody of a guardian. She clarified the question, "Why is he here". The officer then explained; I was arrested for growing marijuana.

To this day I have never seen such a look of hurt and disbelief, as the one that captured my mother's face at that moment. Her reaction caused me to have feelings of guilt and shame that I hoped I would never experience again. Those feelings of guilt grew with time rather than diminishing, primarily as I raised children of my own. As I became disappointed over such small things my children did or didn't do, I would reflect on the magnitude of my actions on that day, and the sorrow my mother must have experienced.

My mother proceeded directly to the fire station where my father was working his 24-hour shift. As my Dad got in the car with a big smile, my Mother told him I had something to tell him. Again, a scene I have tried to compensate for my entire life.

At that time, my hair was several inches down my back. In preparation for the hearing, my mother took me to her friend's hair salon to get a trim. Just before she began, she asked how I would like it cut. With the first clip of the scissors, I realized her question was just polite chatter. I sensed a slight feeling of justice in the air and am sure I would have witnessed a high five had it been period correct at the time.

My parents knew an attorney with an honorable reputation. After telling him the details that lead me to that point, he immediately determined a guilty plea was in order. I was surprised, expecting we could certainly fabricate something to reassign the blame somewhere else. He then coached me on how to address the Judge and present myself. I felt it ridiculous to act so phony, as to use such words as Your Honor and Sir. My parents had taught me how to respectfully address adults; however, my 17 year old prideful vocabulary felt that would be treating him like deity.

The date arrived and we sat on old wood chairs with nothing but faded tile between us and the intimidating courtroom doors. Nervously, I squirmed, feeling so out of place on that felon chair in a new suit that had to be bought for the wrong purpose. Entering the courtroom, flu-like symptoms made it difficult to walk to my dedicated chair. The Judge began by explaining that I could be tried as an adult, because I was 17. That also meant I could serve a term in the federal penitentiary. My heart pounded and my mind was racing. I felt like I was ready to drop off a cliff and the Judge had total control of whether I lived or died. I had never before nor since, felt someone had been given such control over my destiny.

My attorney provided a defense based on the true and sincere stature of my parents, being unable to find anything noteworthy within me. He explained that I, being the 6th of 7 children, was the first to have ever been arrested. The weight of his words caused my head to hang even lower. He asked for leniency based on the fact that I came from a good family, with reputable and caring parents.

After a sobering lecture from the Judge, I was sentenced to one year of probation, with visits to see a probation officer weekly. As the hearing ended I felt a huge relief. I would like to say I learned my lesson and changed forever. Unfortunately, I guess I still had a lot to prove; either to others or myself.

I raise the question, "what drives people to do the things they do"? I am still the same person, but now would avoid jeopardizing my future, or hurting others at any cost. Sure we mature and have more to lose as we get older; but, that jeopardy is not what I am addressing. I just seemed to have such an anger or defiance boiling in me at that time of my life. Then there seemed to be a change that took place within me. It was as if a switch was thrown that turned my life around. It was more than just maturing; it was developing respect and compassion for others. Some people pass their teens and never seem to experience such a change. Others seem to have that type of regard and control of their life the whole time. For myself, there was an absolute change that took place, though the exact cause or very day of that change remains a little speculative. However, I can tell you, a change took place and life has been so much easier and more rewarding since that change.

There are things we can never take back once we have said or done them. As someone who generated such regrettable moments, I would exhort all youth to really think of the consequences of your actions. Every person that has been caught doing something wrong felt they were smart enough to not get caught; or they surely would not have done it. Therefore, if you cannot live with the consequences of getting caught, don't do it. Consequences include seeing pain and sorrow upon your parent's faces, knowing you caused it and you can never take it away. And even if they forgive you, you may never be able to erase it from your mind.

ADDED CONFUSION

I proceeded to experiment with drugs for a short time. There were nights that were very frightening, making me so thankful the next morning, as I awoke normal again. Often feelings of fear, uncertainty, and evilness enveloped me. Sometimes the feelings would be so strong it would scare me toward prayer. I knew I had created quite a mote between God and me; further, I was not sure I could mend our relationship. One evening I offered a prayer in an attempt to initiate some type of movement. I do not know if my eyes were open or closed. I only know that my eyes were suddenly focused on a small dot of light in one corner of the ceiling. That light suddenly began to grow as it drew nearer to me. There was a primary person with a person slightly behind and to each side. They were all dressed in white and had their arms extended as if reaching out to me. It was like they were reaching through a window and I could only see the upper half of their bodies.

This happened very rapidly, and as soon as I realized what I was seeing, they were nearly to me. I suddenly yelled, "I don't want to go yet". Those words came out of my mouth even to my surprise. It was almost as if someone else had spoken and moments later I determined why I had said those words. I guess my immediate thought was, I was dying and someone was coming for me.

No sooner had I spoken those words, and the light vanished. For the next several minutes I lay there, trying to figure out what had just happened. I began to tremble. After ten to fifteen minutes had passed, my father came downstairs and began working in the bathroom next to my bedroom. He later told me he had become very restless in bed and had decided to come downstairs and work on some plumbing he hadn't found the time to repair previously. When my father came down stairs, I wanted to go and tell him what had just happened, but I didn't have the strength to get out of bed for another ten minutes.

When I went into the bathroom, my father was kneeling next to the toilet he was working on. "Are you alright, you look like you've just seen a ghost?" His remark was due to my face being totally white; not aware of just how correct he actually was.

After I explained what I had experienced and I regained my strength, we went up stairs to tell my mother. As we discussed what had transpired, they asked me several questions. My mother asked if I recognized any of the people that had appeared to me. I indicated that no one had looked familiar, especially as briefly as they were there. After some discussion, they neither one had any better idea than I did, as to what had just happened. It was decided that we should kneel and say a prayer, that we may get some resolve. My father prayed, asking that we might know the purpose of the experience.

The night ended without gaining any idea as to why it had taken place. One thing that did happen was that I was afraid to say a prayer for a long, long time. And I especially didn't pray when alone or in the dark.

Years passed and from time to time I would wonder what I was to have received from that night. I fasted and prayed several times that I would know what message I was to have received or if I was to have been taken. At times I had been closer to the Spirit than others. During the times I felt closest to God, I would ask for the answer to those questions. At other times, when I had done things contrary to the Spirit of God, my dad would ask me how I could do such things, having had that visitation. That experience left me with more fear and questions than understanding. I didn't really feel it to be a blessing from God. The years of unanswered prayers about that night left me wondering if it happened because I was a bad person or a good person. I did; however, know for a certainty that there was another realm amongst us, withheld by a veil.

My life teetered between darkness and light. Each time I tried to redirect my life toward righteousness; I would again feel an evil presence begin to build around me. It would become so intense, day and night, that I would turn the other direction, with confirmed feelings that God could not save me from the darkness. After reverting back to a life of unrighteous living and void of prayer, the darkness would subside once again. My spiral continued down a path that seemed out of my control. One afternoon, I got into an altercation and Battery charges were filed against me. Luckily, I had earlier removed a pistol from my trunk, or the outcome may have been dramatically worse. Appearing in court alone, I represented myself; with no additional credibility. My nervousness was dampened by my unfortunate familiarity of the environment. I received probation once again for a year. What a blessing I didn't have the gun in the car that day. Realizing I didn't learn much about packing weapons in the seventh grade, I permanently refrained from carrying a gun in my car.

A short time later my friend Roger borrowed my truck for the evening. Without my knowledge, he used it for a burglary. When the police responded to an alarm at the bar next to his parent's house, they found my truck sitting in the dark. He managed to crawl out the back window and through the manure filled cow pasture, to stinking freedom. They didn't catch him, but with his history in the area and being my roommate they highly suspected he did it. The police held my truck as evidence for about three weeks; hoping I would turn him in. They finally gave my truck back; at which time I drove Roger to Canada. He returned for Christmas in a stolen truck several months later. A few years after that, some things from his past caught up to him, sending him to prison. Unfortunately it was after he had straightened up and had a wife and two children.

During the same period of time I had gotten addicted to amphetamines for about six months. With three roommates, our apartment was often the location of late night parties. Not able to get much sleep at night and up at 4 AM for work at a dairy, I turned to drugs just to keep going. The drugs kept me going; but prevented me from wanting to eat. I was 5'8'' and weighed 125 pounds, down from 155. Much of the time, I not only wasn't hungry; but felt sick. I had been so sick on nearly every kind of alcohol, that I couldn't drink anything except beer. The word partying should evoke an image in your mind of joy and fun. But when I look back on that time of my life, I can't seem to recall any joy or happiness. A gloom seemed to surround me, with no apparent escape route in site.

This is a small list of the things that put me over the line that many never return from. Although I feared the Lord couldn't save me; how hard He must have been working to protect me from myself. He did not allow me to fail or pay the severe consequences that were appropriate. For this reason, I feel it is my obligation to witness as to how forgiving and caring the Lord actually is. Many people feel they have sinned too greatly to be forgiven and are afraid to pray and ask for forgiveness. This is just Satan keeping you from the truth.

This is not intended to focus on the negative or dark times in my life. I only mention a small portion of them to show how confused I was and how distant the Spirit of God had to have been, as I was trying to find my direction. And I am reminded every time my mind dares to look back at that dark period of my life, just how immense the Atonement of Jesus Christ is.

THE IGNITION

Many of my early adult years were spent seeking a testimony of God the Father, Jesus Christ and whether or not the religion of my childhood could help me accomplish that. From my late teens I began feeling insulted by individuals as they verbally attacked my basic and limited beliefs. They did not confront me directly, so they could not have known they were in some way being disrespectful of my religious foundation. My lifestyle and actions would not have given them the slightest indication their words could possibly be offensive to my ears. And the absence of any words expelled from my own mouth did not cut short any of their reveling in unchallenged bigotry.

By dating, the number of people doubled that would unknowingly offend my beliefs without ever realizing it. By marrying, the list suddenly expanded beyond my own connections, to include in-laws, wife's coworkers and friends. There seemed to be no shortage of people willing to attack the things I believed in. The difficulty of being able to say anything in retaliation also increased, as many of the relationships in my life were no longer mine alone, to eliminate or distance myself from.

To be perfectly honest; however, it was not the complexity of relationships, my not being an exemplar of my beliefs, nor was it my non-confrontational nature that caused me to sit like a mute as unchecked bashing encircled me. In those days, it was because I was not converted to my childhood beliefs, I did not know my Savior, and my Father in Heaven was an obscure image in various pictures I had seen while growing up. Although I was often personally angered by religious bashing, I did not speak up because I would not know what to say. I could not defend nor testify of truths through the use of scriptural or historical references. I could not give examples of Christ's organizational structure and the foundational beliefs He personally established during His ministry on earth. It wasn't that those things didn't exist; it was that I could not produce them if I provoked an exchange with anyone. Therefore, I found it easier to leave the area and find another group to mingle with if possible. If that wasn't an option, I would sit with an artificial grin as I mentally drafted a list of things I needed answers to.

My wife and I did not share in a common religion. Although she did not have a solid conviction of another religion, she did have concerns about certain aspects of my beliefs. There were many co-workers, family members, and friends that continued to give her numberless reasons to distance herself from such beliefs. A number of those individuals were former members of my own church; which seemed to give her credence for their concerns. That puzzled me, as their experiences and knowledge somehow held more weight and validity than my own.

All those uncomfortable encounters of religious bashing did not cause me to pursue the knowledge I was so lacking. And the feeling of religious incompetency my wife surely had for me, caused little more than an itch to begin growing within me. Even the unavoidable reality often debated within myself, that I was not actually converted to such truths myself, did little to move me forward. Instead I continued a lifestyle contrary to where I knew I needed to go.

One afternoon, I stood in the sunshine admiring the awakening of beautiful flowers and green grass in my front yard. Little did I know, that carefree feeling of springtime bliss was about to be cut short. I stood with a smile on my face and my faithful dog by my side, in front of our little house built for two, as my wife pulled to the curb in our little blue two-door Datsun B210. She got out of the car and after a brief exchange she said the rabbit died. I had no idea what she was talking about. She told me she just came from the doctor's office and her pregnancy was confirmed. Those words caused nearly an out of body experience within me. I clearly heard the words in my mind **"and the sins of the child will be upon the head of the father"**. A whirlwind of things I needed to change in my life began rolling through my mind. The swirling would pause as each item was clearly presented, then the spinning would begin until the next item was presented. A number of things were clearly shown before I suddenly heard my wife's voice in my ears. **"I am glad you are so excited"**, her words trailing off, as she was already several steps toward the house. I have no idea how long I glazed over before she began walking away, but it was long enough to require a lot of damage control.

My wife and I had been married for over four years before she got pregnant. Although we had developed a strong bond during our marriage, I feel that is the day our lives suddenly had purpose. There wasn't the slightest regret or hesitation; although, she may have initially thought otherwise. Our unity was instantaneous, our resolve was to be the best we could be, and our focus became outward rather than inward. My responsibility became so profound that very day. For months, I experienced great internal battles; causing me to look as a fool, while standing in front of the beer selection. However, I never did drink from that day forward. And I began a serious search to find God and what He would have me do.

There comes a time in many people's lives, that they question their handed down parent's knowledge and beliefs. For me that came to a head the day my wife told me she was pregnant. Prior to that day, I had risked destroying my life in so many ways. I was bewildered and uncertain of what God's plan was for me and whether He had the **ability** to save me from Satan's grasp. However, with all my careless actions, I again mention that the Lord protected me and caused results far better than I deserved.

A LONG SOUGHT ANSWER

My wife and I attended my brother's wedding in Northern Idaho, shortly before our daughter was born. Having grown up in Southern Idaho, I could not believe Coeur d' Alene was in the same state. The gorgeous lake and beautiful pines were so inviting that it caused a desire within my wife and I to move there. After a year of planning, I relocated with our belongings, while my wife and daughter remained back in Pocatello, pending a transfer with her work.

My life had been set on a new path with my wife's pregnancy. I had actively attended church for nearly two years. After moving to Coeur d' Alene alone, diligent scripture reading accompanied with regular prayers was unlike anything I had ever done. That I did partly in hopes of filling the void of my wife and young daughter not being with me; but, I was also driven to find answers that continued to elude me. Never before had I felt such peace in my life. There were so many things I read in scripture; which, the Spirit of God confirmed within me. A foundational understanding of God and His Gospel were etched upon my heart, leaving man's simple reasoning no fracture to burrow in. My individual confirmation had taken place, in what I would call a 'logical conversion'.

It had been twelve to fourteen years since the visitation I had experienced during my youth. My subconscious seemed to cross check everything against that experience and require verification through prayer. My sister had recently sent me a life sketch of my paternal grandmother. She was such a wonderful loving person and my mind was flooded with wonderful memories of time spent with her when I was a child. I sat alone that evening reading through the pages. Turning to a new page, there was a photograph of my grandmother's grandfather. As my eyes settled on that picture, it was as if someone shouted in my ear, with great excitement. The words were short, plain, and simple, "It's him". I immediately knew it was in reference to the visitation I had received so long ago.

The picture disappeared as my eyes filled with tears. My heart felt like it was going to explode with excitement. At last, I had finally received the answer as to who had visited me that night. I didn't really know why he had come, but I knew who it was at last. Even though I felt such joy and certainty at finally knowing who had visited me, I felt I needed to get confirmation from God. I knelt down and began to say a prayer. Having barely begun, I asked if in fact, this was the person that had come to me in my room that night. At that instant, every bit of excitement left me. I don't remember hearing the word "no", but I felt it. There wasn't any disappointment, or further question in my heart. I knelt for probably another minute, trying to think of another word to say. My mind could not generate a single word. I could not even find an "Amen" to close my prayer with. I no longer wonder what is meant by a stupor of thought.

With the inability to find another word, I also instantly knew the original visitation I had received, while in my teens, had been a visitation of an evil nature[1]. Without saying another word or even closing my prayer, I returned to the couch. I again began to read the genealogy. After I read for a short time, my mind strayed as I began analyzing the events that had just transpired.

---

[1] Evil spirits and even Satan deceives - D&C 50:2

As I thought about the original visitation, and the experience that had just taken place, I gained some very powerful insights that have helped me in a number of situations throughout my life. It helped me to understand the power of prayer and the importance of using the correct methods while praying.

As we are taught to pray, we are told to ask God for confirmation of our decisions. We are not to just ask for directions; but are to make a decision on what we feel is the right choice. Then through prayer, ask the Lord if our decision is the right one. If the answer is yes, we may feel excited and feel good about our decision. If it is the wrong decision, we may have a stupor of thought.

The night of the original visitation, to the best of my knowledge, my father had prayed that we might know the reason for the visitation. I do not believe he ever asked if I was to have been taken that night; which was my belief and fear for a number of years. And for years, I fasted and prayed that I might know what message was to have been gained that night. At no time did I ask if that visitation was of God. That should probably have been the very first question that was asked. I also did not directly ask if I was to have been taken that night. That was another question that I should have sought the answer to. However, I may not have been living worthy enough to receive an answer during most of my days before that evening.

I am not saying that God can only answer us if we word things just so, because I know that He is capable of anything that He desires. But, if we ask questions, in a manner that requires conversive-type answers, what are the chances we will receive an answer? We would need a visitation or detailed dream to gain that type of answer. In contrast, if we ask close ended questions that require a straight yes or no, how much more likely are we to receive an answer? With that type of question, we can receive what is described in the scriptures as a burning within our heart, knowing of its truth or a stupor of thought[2], knowing the thing is wrong.

The first thing the visitation did was to scare me so bad that I ceased praying for over a year. The second was that it left me confused. If God has a message important enough to send a messenger through the veil, you will receive that message. I don't think the messenger will turn around and leave because you say you don't want it, or don't want to go with them. Can you picture the messenger going back and reporting that his mission didn't go to well, because someone just didn't want the information or want to return with them?

The original visitation confused me, and its purpose eluded me for so many years. After receiving an answer the night I viewed the photograph and prayed about it, I have had no disappointment or fear. The answer was so definite and absolute, burned deep within my soul, as a witness from the Spirit will be. It increased my awareness that Satan will go to any measure to get one individual to follow him. He will entice us and deceive us in any manner that he can. He will play on our fears and the things that are most important to us. He is very patient and has a long-range plan. It does not matter to him how long it takes if he is successful at securing someone's future for eternity.

Satan is the master of deceit. Whoever visited me that night was all in white, which we associate with God or angels[3]. My face wasn't radiant, but was white from fear. When I thought I had received a long sought answer to my prayers, I felt great joy and excitement. That is, right up until I asked God to confirm those feelings.

Therefore, I feel Satan is capable of stirring up the same feelings within you as God does. However, God will discern right from wrong, if you seek Him in prayer. In earnest prayer, Satan is not allowed to confound and confuse.

---

[2] Stupor of thought and burning heart - D&C 9:7, Knock and it will be opened - 3 Nephi 27:29, Hearts burned - Luke 24:32
[3] 2Nephi 9:9

This makes it evident to me, that even when searching for religion, one must have knowledge of the subject, allowing them to ask educated questions. They can then approach God in prayer for confirmation to their questions. If you seek answers, other than through prayer, Satan has the means to intervene.

Satan can deceive and convince people of falsehoods. Even after crucifying Christ and receiving signs; such as: the Earth darkening for three days, quakes, etc.; people remained convinced they did not kill their Savior. Their ancestors, to this day, may believe or admit that Christ was a wise man, maybe even a prophet, but nothing more.

If Christ was only a prophet, He would have been a false prophet. Declaring He was the Savior, the Son of God, he would have been deceiving the people if He were only a prophet. Therefore, Christ was either the Savior or a deceiver. Holding true to the doctrine of the Bible, "That that is not of God, is of Satan". Satan is the father of deceit, and deceit is not found in any of God's doctrine. Therefore, if we were to say Christ was a deceiver, we would be saying he was one of Satan's workers on this Earth, here to lead God the Father's children away from Him.

Knowing of Christ's mission on this Earth and the love and light He has poured upon me, I can't imagine anyone not really being able to determine which role Christ actually filled while on this Earth.

There are a lot of things written by people that have had visitations of angels or even of the Lord. It would make me feel a lot better to be able to say I was deserving of such a visitation. However, I have not received any such thing, wondering for years why I was allowed to receive such a scary and direct intervention from such an evil and deceiving entity. I can only say that it was as real as my father was in the next room. And I hope I will never again let myself be deceived or fear the power of Satan. I know that Satan will try to convince people of his power, even to the convincing that he can utterly destroy all the Saints and gain God's glory. He will be able to convince his followers, right up until they encircle the extremely outnumbered Saints at the final battle of Armageddon. At that time, they will be shown that sheer numbers and perceived power, is no match for God and a smaller group of Saints endowed with His strength.

Chapter 6

THE MINER

Later, during that same year in Coeur d' Alene, I again found myself alone, as my wife and daughter were visiting family in Pocatello. One evening I had a dream that was a very profound experience and one that I am yet to fully understand forty years later.

In the dream: I was jogging on a dirt road lined with sagebrush and June grass in an unrecognizable desert. Two people I had graduated from high school with, were jogging with me. One of them was my best friend and the other was a girl that grew up in the same church as I did, who was a good friend of my cousin's. As we were jogging, the wind began to blow. We could not feel the wind, but the sound was penetrating. The gusting whispers of the wind became louder, causing us to stop to better hear. We turned, facing eastward toward the near-by cedar covered hill; that seeming to be the direction of the wind.

Turning back toward the south we noticed two people a short distance up the road. One was an old miner sitting on a large rock just off to the left side of the road. His overalls and shirt dirty from a long day of work, his hard hat and light still upon his head. The light and coal dust upon his face testified of the dark dreary work environment in which he had spent much of his time. Sorrow streamed from him in waves as he heaved with agony from deep within his soul. A younger miner, fresh to the occupation it appeared, stood trying to console, with no success. The sound we had thought to be wind was actually the old miner crying. His words suddenly clear as he sobbed, "I don't want to die". It seemed to go on forever, his voice cutting deeply into my heart. I could feel his pain and sorrow; his great fear of dying so tangible.

My eyes were drawn to an approaching car, still some distance away. The dust swirled from the sides of the car as it barreled down a hill, closing the gap between us. Arriving, it pulled to a stop next to my friends and me. We didn't hesitate as the three of us piled into the back seat of the car. In the dream I knew the people in the front seat, but I never really saw who it was. I just remember so clearly how thankful I was to just get out of the reach of that penetrating voice. Still in the dream, suddenly I was standing, talking to my brother's father-in-law. As I described what we had seen while we were jogging, he just commented, "Those old miners just get awful lonely out there". Then I woke up from the dream.

It was just before 5 am when I awoke. Though awake, the effects of that piercing voice were still very vivid, leaving me shaken while I lay in bed. I tried to figure out what any of it meant. The deep sorrow the miner felt transferred to me, pushing me from my bed to my knees, seeking the comfort he was unable to find. I asked God that I might be comforted and that I might understand any meaning the dream may hold.

Returning to my bed after closing the prayer, I began to evaluate the dream. I suddenly realized the old miner was my brother's great uncle by marriage. He was an uncle to my brother's father in-law. That uncle had actually worked in the mines in Butte, Montana and Wallace, Idaho, while he was growing up. He was now an old man and lived across town by himself. The younger miner was my brother's father in law, Jess, who worked briefly in the Wallace mine early in his work career.

I tried to go back to sleep, but I couldn't. Before I knew it, I was taking a shower and getting dressed. While my body got ready to go over to Uncle Paul's house, my mind was trying to build a case of how stupid that would be. It was way too early to knock on someone's door and what would I tell him, when and if he answered? It didn't seem to matter, because I found myself sitting in my car in front of his house. I then decided I would just go to the door and see if I could hear anyone stirring. If it didn't sound like anyone was up, I would simply go back home.

As I approached the door, I began to hear something coming from inside. It was the same sound that I had heard while facing that cedar cover hill in my dream. A muffled voice coming through the door sounded just as the wind did. As I got to the door, the voice became clear. While now standing at the door, I could hear Uncle Paul clearly sobbing, "I don't want to die". The voice was so clear and was identical to what I had heard in my dream.

I knocked and it seemed like an eternity before he opened the door. Without hesitation he invited me in, with fresh tears still on his cheeks. With no denial possible, he began as if nothing was out of the ordinary. He told me that he was going in for some tests that morning and that he was afraid he had cancer. His blunt opening made it feel as though our discourse had been much longer already. Then he continued talking for quite some time, telling me about all those years he watched his wife die, and how heartbreaking it was to take care of her and see her in so much pain. He expressed so much bitterness toward doctors, hospitals, and research organizations. "After contributing to them for years, they didn't do anything to help save my wife", he explained. They simply told him they couldn't do anything for her. Passing through the enduring experience of losing his wife, caused him to become an atheist after her death.

Suddenly I knew why I was there. It wasn't easy; but, I asked that self-titled atheist if he would like me to say a prayer with him. In an almost defeated and conceding tone, he simply replied, "That would be fine". After we prayed, he seemed to calm considerably. I wasn't there to talk to him, but to listen. He poured out his heart for a considerable amount of time. Can you imagine the fear he must have felt; having witnessed what his wife had gone through and not having anyone to talk to, including God? During all that time, he never really questioned why I was out at that time of day or why I had just stopped by.

As I returned home, it became evident what had transpired and how blessed I was to have been part of that wonderful experience. It was also clear as to why my two friends were in the dream. I had failed to share the gospel with each of them when I had the opportunity to. My friend was not a member and my cousin's girlfriend was only an active member in her school years. I think she was a member primarily for the social aspect. Years after we graduated I saw her and she was struggling after a failed relationship. She seemed so alone and didn't know where to turn. I felt the prompting to tell her that Christ was there waiting, but feeling awkward I failed to say anything.

For the next fifteen years I thought of that experience often. I had tried to believe that I missed my opportunity to discuss the Church with each of them. And by then, they would have heard about it from someone else if it were so important for them to hear it.

Just as real as the dream of the miner was, it was then made known to me that the responsibility was still on my shoulders. One afternoon as I drove to Beaver, UT., I began to think about the dream of many years prior. As I was almost to Fillmore, I said a prayer in my heart; thanking God for that and the many other great experiences I had been blessed with. As the events that took place in the dream were going through my mind, I glanced out of my side window in the eastern direction. As I viewed the hills, I experienced the most peaceful feeling. It felt like seeing your home on the horizon at the conclusion of a long journey. Those hills were identical to the ones in my dream. I looked back at the road in disbelief, thinking I had just imagined that they were similar. As I gained my composure, I looked back at the hills. The same peaceful feeling came over me and I knew that it was the place in my dream. I had driven past that location a number of times over the years, but I had never noticed those hills, and that place had no special significance to me prior to that day.

I really wanted to get off the freeway and drive toward the hills, but I had an appointment to meet someone in Beaver. After my appointment, I returned to Fillmore. I exited the freeway just outside of Fillmore by the hills I had noticed earlier. It felt like I was on an Easter egg hunt. I began trying to find the dirt road I had seen in my dream. Within minutes I crossed a dirt road that ran parallel to the hills. The road and hills looked very familiar. The thought of Close Encounters came across my mind. Amusing, as it seemed, I felt the need to walk up the dirt road. As I walked up the dirt road, I began to feel very uncomfortable. A very strong feeling of anxiety came over me. I began to wonder if I was going crazy and had fabricated the whole thing. The fear of someone coming and harming me began to seem very real.

As I stood on the dirt road and prayed for comfort and confirmation, that I might know if I was there for a reason, an old truck pulled up next to mine and stopped. I cut my prayer short and began walking toward my truck. My heart was pounding like it did when I was a child, running past the empty field toward my house in the dark of night. As I began to walk the truck took off. When I was almost to my truck, I noticed a large rock that looked familiar in some way. When I backed my truck up to leave, I again noticed the rock in my mirror. It was like it meant something to me, but I didn't know what it was.

I returned home with a renewed excitement that the Lord still heard my prayers and knew that I existed. I also realized that Satan seemed to distract me or utilize fear, whenever God was in the middle of a powerful teaching moment. But it held true, that through prayer, Satan's perceived power was defused once again.

That evening I pulled my old journal from the shelf. The original dream had happened so long ago, that I felt a desire to read what I had originally written. My memory was that we had met the miner while the two men were walking down the road. I had forgotten that he was actually sitting on a large rock while the other man stood next to him. My written story brought the vivid image back to my mind intact.

My dream was no longer just a dream in my mind, but became a very real place that I have stood. The events and locations I have now experienced in person. Therefore, I know it was something very real and important to my Father in Heaven. There was something that was made clear to me that day also. God does not physically do some things in this world. He uses us to accomplish his work here. I knew that I could not rid my mind of this, until I fulfilled my obligation. And I knew I certainly did not want to die and face God, knowing that I had not acted on the promptings I had received for so many years regarding this matter.

I do not push my beliefs on anyone else. My religion has always been very special to me, and I love to share it with anyone who is interested. But I do not feel comfortable trying to debate its truthfulness with someone that only wants to tear it down. I know that the Lord had a reason I had not been allowed to put all of that behind me. The words of James Faust in the 1996 fall conference rang in my ears. He told of a time he put off apologizing to his grandmother. It had haunted him for years, as she died before he took the time to set things right.

I knew in my heart that I needed to write to my two friends in the dream. There was a real need to share the dream and my testimony with them. Years later I saw my friend at a school class reunion. I wondered what he would say. I had indicated that I would not mention it again when I saw him, but wanted him to read my testimony and the Book of Mormon I sent him.

After we briefly talked he thanked me for the message I had sent. I told him I was not sure what he would think, but that I needed to do it. He said it must have been hard, but thanked me for doing it. I have not been able to locate my cousin's friend, but will continue to try. I feel I have done my work and will now let the Lord do His.

Years later I went on a trip with my younger brother. He had spent a couple days prior to us meeting in Fillmore, visiting the area and trying to find the burial locations of our Great Grandparents. He had found a couple locations that were significant to their lives; which were located several miles west of the dirt road that was in my dream. I took him there the next day and showed him that spot as I told him and his son of my dream and how I found that same place many years later. I am not sure if or how that all ties to our Great Grandparents and other family members formerly living in the area, but I am sure I will someday understand it all.

Chapter 7

A YEAR FROM HELL

Prior to our move to Coeur d' Alene, my wife and I had been married for five years. We both made good money and didn't seem to want for anything. We had a dog named Zac that understood conversation and directions better than a lot of people I have worked with. As we discussed having our first child, my wife and I were both in fear that we may never love a child as much as we loved our dog.

Not long after our daughter was born, we found ourselves booting the dog out of the path of the baby's walker. It is truly amazing how the instant bond of parenting consumes your entire life; from the first moment you hold that tiny little soul, fresh from the arms of our Father in Heaven. As active and busy as we both were our world ground to a halt and everything in our lives was altered and began to revolve around our new daughter. I have always had a low tolerance for just sitting around. Always on the move, I was either out doing some physical entertainment, working one or two side jobs, or spending my time on some project in the garage. With the presence of a beautiful new baby girl, I found myself content to just sit and hold that little bundle for hours.

Our move from Pocatello, Idaho to Coeur d' Alene wasn't a spur of the moment decision; but was one of the most thought out and planned moves we have ever made. While attending my brother's wedding there a year earlier, we immediately fell in love with the area. From that time we began to make adjustments to someday be able to move there.

My brother and I decided we would both move our new families at the same time. Planning to start a new drywall business, we went to check on work availability, housing, and develop an overall strategy. We successfully landed a drywall job on a large custom home, nestled in the pines with a fantastic view. While working on that home I envisioned my own family living in such a beautiful setting. That week my desire to move there became the absolute next step that had to happen in our lives. It no longer seemed like an option; but now felt like destiny. That week we also talked to a number of other building contractors. They seemed excited to have a new drywall company coming to town. We returned home with confidence that we would have plenty of work when we returned.

As the annual winter slumber of construction settled in, we felt it a perfect time to move north. When the following spring arrived we had hoped to be ready for the on-slot of new spring construction.

After arriving, eagerly we hit the streets to revisit all those contractors we had met during our initial trip. Before midday arrived, our visions of bliss began to show sever fractures. It seemed everyone we talked to was just finishing their last unsold home and had no plans of starting more until all were sold. Since it was their last home, no one felt comfortable trusting their drywall to a couple of strangers.

Although we were able to land a few jobs, the work did not start normally that particular spring. The extended construction slump was later identified as the 1979 recession. Things became very bleak in that area of the country. First all the mining shut down and then the lumber mills shut down; which, in turn brought the construction industry to a halt. The drought in work caused us to take any work associated to a paycheck.

While working on a small remodel we coordinated our work with the painting contractor. His work quality and ethics were of such high standards, being unusual and yet refreshingly familiar. My brother and I learned to finish drywall and paint under the direction of our father. My father was one of many in his family to learn the trades from their father. I have made feeble attempts to always uphold the impeccable quality and honesty my family had been known for through generations. Therefore, it was a joy to work with that painter; which took me back to days of working with my father. His acquaintance eventually evolved into us being employed by him. Later, my brother worked for him on a steady basis.

When we first moved to the area we purchased ten acres of wooded property on which we planned to each build a house. It was some distance north of Coeur d Alene, near Spirit Lake. My wife and I found the perfect place to situate our house in a small clearing on the back part of the timbered lot. We visited there several times and imagined life in our new home. The image is still vivid in my mind of my wife and daughter standing next to a tall tree on that beautiful piece of ground. However, the reality we found ourselves in caused us to sell the ground and practicality forced us to by a lot in Coeur d' Alene. By building in town we obtained a building lot for less money, didn't have to pay to drill a well, and travel to work on the house was more feasible.

The 10 acres sold quickly after we put it up for sale; which provided a down payment for a new building lot. We finally felt like we were moving forward. Our plan was to move into the house at completion. If things remained slow, we could sell the house and basically recoup my wages for working on the house. Surely the slow economy wouldn't last too long!

We paid off the lot with the construction loan as well as all the building material and foundation costs. I had become friends and worked with a very talented and hard working man. Tom and I had a lot of common skills. He also taught and helped me with the ones I didn't already know. With his help, I did everything on that house after it was framed up.

Every day after I completed work on any customer jobs, I would go work on the house until the early morning hours. If I didn't have any other work, I would work 16-hour days on the house.
As completion of the house neared, we had made the decision to move back to Pocatello. It seemed that as beautiful as it was in Coeur d' Alene, it wasn't very enjoyable when one's situation was as bleak as ours. My wife put in for a transfer back to Pocatello.

One day as I was traveling to work on the house, I stopped at the lumberyard. When I came out of the lumberyard, I was going to go to my friend's house a couple of blocks away. Needing to turn left toward his house, it was as if I had a momentary lapse of what I was doing. Turning right, I noticed an automobile accident in the intersection ahead. In the middle of the intersection sat a yellow Volkswagen. Neither the police nor paramedics were yet on the scene. I stopped my truck and started walking toward the Volkswagen. My brother's mother-in-law drove a car that looked just like that car. As I hesitantly approached the car I hoped it wasn't her. Looking in the car, a wave of total disbelief rolled over me. There Penny was, her legs trapped under the driver side dashboard and her upper body slumped over onto the passenger's seat. The dull round shifter knob had been rammed through her leg close to her knee. She seemed lifeless at first; but began moaning and trying to talk as I spoke to her. After identifying myself, she began asking what had happened. She was in indescribable pain and could not move. I ran back to the lumber store to place a phone call to emergency services.

The ambulance arrived rapidly. One crew began working on her and the other crew was across the highway working on the individuals from the other car that had run the stop sign. The driver of the other car had been thrown from his vehicle and was laying in the median.

At the hospital, a considerable amount of time passed before the doctors emerged from the operating room. Finally one of them came and gave the family a report. Penny had a broken sternum, both legs were broken in numerous places, her jaw was broke in several places. They said her condition would require months of surgeries and hospitalization. My brother and I were able to give her a blessing. Even though she and her family were not members of the LDS church, they felt a prayer of any type could not hurt. In the following days the doctor took several more x-rays. He later reported that he must have read the earlier x-rays incorrectly, as he could only find a portion of the breaks he had identified earlier. Once again the subtle miracles and blessings of the Lord can be explained away, or we can choose to see the Lord's hand in answering our prayers. This isn't to say that the road ahead wasn't still a very rough one and from some injuries she never fully recovered. But, I would think the reduction of breaks and damage was surely a blessing.

During the car crash, Penny had a near death experience. She told us of being above the scene of the accident and described the car she hit, where it was sitting, and described seeing the paramedics working on someone laying in the median. This would have been impossible to see from her vantage point while lying in her car. As they removed her from her car, a collar was placed on her neck and I for one, saw that she never had a chance to look around at the accident scene before they rushed her off in the ambulance. She also described talking to her deceased mother and father while floating above the chaotic scene below. She watched as they loaded her body into the ambulance. After her mother informed her, it was not yet time for her to go, she was immediately captured within her broken body and suddenly felt the immense pain from severe injuries. Over the next couple of months I was able to visit this wonderfully strong lady in the hospital. She was always positive and such a sweet person, even then worried she was inconveniencing those that came to see her.

Things were awfully quiet and lonely around her house without her there. Her husband was home alone and I know it was very difficult on him. They had asked if we would stay there until we moved back to Pocatello. We gladly accepted and hoped that having our companionship and our toddler's entertaining presence would help remove some of the silence and gloom from his long evenings.

Just before moving back to Pocatello, my wife had felt a lump on the inside of her gum, by her back tooth. She went to a dentist who evaluated the situation. He determined it didn't appear to be anything serious. Rather than traveling with a sore mouth, he advised her to go see a surgeon, after she moved in the coming weeks. Following his advisement, she went to a surgeon when she returned to Pocatello. He determined he should remove the lump and verify its nature. At the conclusion of the surgery he gave her good news. From the appearance of the tumor, there appeared to be nothing to worry about. As with any biopsy or removal, he sent the specimen off for final evaluation by a lab.

I was nearing the completion of the house back in Coeur d' Alene. All I had left to do was the exterior painting and to pour concrete sidewalks and porches. I scheduled to have a realtor give me an estimate of the value and set up the listing. As she walked through the house, she commented on the quality and appeal it offered. Completing her tour, she quoted me a price she felt the house might sell for. I can imagine how bleached my face must have suddenly appeared. In disbelief I confirmed the price with her. Now I really knew I was going to be sick. She then informed me of the realty fees that would be coming out of that figure if they were able to sell it. "The market is really quite slow and we may not be able to get that amount", she continued.

Ushering her to the door I barely responded. I wasn't trying to be rude; but, was feeling quite sick and couldn't even find the composure to carry on the conversation further. After closing the door behind her, I slowly began walking from room to room in nearly a trance. Her estimated selling price just kept rolling through my head. It basically meant that if the house sold for top dollar, I would break even after paying off the loan, and would then have to pay over $6,000 in realtor commission out of my pocket.

As I went in one room after another, I began recalling all the work and dedication that each room contained. I thought of all the many late nights spent pulling wire, plumbing and insulating. My mind recalled the cold winter days, while putting on siding. I pictured myself sliding down the roof twice, as I tried to remove the box of nails frozen to the roof's surface, cutting and installing frozen shingles, installing the furnace and all the duct work. I remembered feeling such excitement as the house took shape during the drywall stages. I had installed every light, sink and tub; then the house grew in beauty as finish trim, cabinets, paint and carpet created a house more wonderful than anything I thought I would ever live in.

The more I reflected the more upset I got. I could possibly have accepted just breaking even and consider myself lucky for all the experience I had gained. But the idea of working every spare minute for nearly six months, just to turn around and give a realtor half of my entire salary for that year didn't have much appeal. Even if I felt good about it, I didn't have a clue how I could gather such an amount of money.

It was about 4 o'clock in the afternoon; but suddenly seemed as dark as the middle of the night. I walked around the house and locked all the doors and windows. Walking over to my only possession that I had placed in that house, I turned up the stereo to a nearly ear bleed volume. Sitting on the floor in the hallway, I was out of view of any of the bare windows. I could no longer hold back the emotions that seemed to explode within me. As I thought of all the events of that trying year, the house just became a fitting end. Knowing I could not be seen or heard from outside the house, my emotions ran free. I swore, cried, and rolled around on the floor in an uncontrolled rage. My feelings rolled through disbelief, pity, anger and back again. This continued until I was nearly exhausted and could barely pull myself from the floor.

Eventually I made it to the front door. After briefly looking back into the house, I pulled the door shut. As I got to my car, I paused again, I stood for several minutes looking at the house, as if separating myself from a loved one, about to begin a long departure.

I got home and felt lifeless and defeated. About an hour had passed before I received a phone call from my wife. She too was very upset and through a tearful, struggling voice, asked if I would come home to Pocatello. I indicated I still had a couple of weeks of work left, before the house would be completed. Feeling that was not the right opportunity to elaborate on the realtor's disclosure, I asked her for more details about her request. Knowing we had been separated before for greater amounts of time, and she being a strong and independent person, I felt there must be more to the story. She then informed me that after further testing by the lab, they determined the tumor removed from her mouth was malignant. Requiring a second surgery, she wanted me home as soon as possible.

In a flash the house became a very minor issue in my life. I assured her I would be there the next afternoon. As I lay in bed alone that night, darkness seemed to swallow my world. I offered sporadic incomplete prayers, between the sobs and jumbled reasoning. It felt like an eternity before I began to see daylight slowly crepe through the window. During those endless hours of darkness, my wife's phone call replayed over and over in my mind. Hundreds of attempts were unsuccessful at rationally organizing a plan to satisfy the endless loose ends that had instantaneously been created in a matter of minutes the evening before. Suddenly the beaming morning light caused things to become very clear, as my life was suddenly put into perspective for me. I realized the importance of family and our relationships with one another. I also realized the non-importance of possessions in this life that can be taken from us at any time; ripped from our grip as we find ourselves thrust toward our next existence.

As I arrived at the airport it was so great to see my wife. We gave each other an embrace that was more than just hello. A sobering reality had come over us; we had no guarantee we would always be there for each other. A quick glimpse had suddenly caused us to realize we were mortal and all the hopes and plans for a long life together, were suddenly no longer a given. I know everyone knows there are no guarantees, but that isn't the same understanding as what was just awakened in each of us. After we were finally able to pull ourselves apart, we headed for home.

Home was a very loose term at that point. My wife had moved in with her parents, and was planning to stay there until I finished the house in Cour d Alene and returned to Pocatello. Her parents were so gracious, as were so many people during that time. They kept insisting that there would be a lot of house sitting empty if we weren't staying there. We stayed with them for a number of months, until we were able to determine where we were headed with our lives.

My wife had a second surgery and then received radiation treatments. The second surgery was required, because they felt they weren't as cautious as they should have been the first time, as the original tumor didn't appear to be malignant. Before taking her into surgery, they prepared us for the worse. My wife was informed of all the complications that could take place. Then they pulled me aside and covered some greater issues with me. I was told that due to the location of the tumor, some major problems existed. The tumor was located on the inside edge of the jawbone, right by the rear molar. They would have to go in from the inside of her mouth as well as work from the outside of her neck. There was not a lot of room to work in and if there appeared to be any malignant matter left, it could result in some serious complications. One of the main arteries going to the brain runs through the area so they couldn't do much with that immediate area if it had spread or attached to anything else. They said they might have to remove some of her jawbone if the cancer had attached to the bone. There were also major nerves in the area that could leave her with major distortion and paralysis on one side of her face. I was asked to prepare for the worst and they also asked if I could still love her if she was severely disfigured. They told me she was going to need my love and support if things turned out bad. I asked them to do everything they could do to save her and I would love her no matter what the outcome was.

When finally alone with her in the room I gave her a priesthood blessing. I remember wishing I could just tell her that everything would be fine. But I did feel impressed to tell her that the doctors would be guided in what they were to do. I also told her that if it be the will of God, that she would fully recover. I don't think she gained a lot of assurance or calming from the blessing, at least not to the degree I did. As I finished the blessing, it was as if I knew things would be all right. It was kind of like knowing what your Christmas present is, but you don't want to celebrate too early, just in case it doesn't come through for some reason.

As she emerged from surgery, things looked quite well. They informed me that it did seem to be a success. She did lose all the lymph nodes on one side of her neck, some saliva glands, and a small section of the back of her tongue. Her tongue was cut and then attached to her jaw. This limited her ability to move her tongue, which caused her to have to learn how to talk all over. She did have a great plastic surgeon, so the external scars were under her jaw and very hard to detect. There was a slight indention on the one side of her neck from the loss of the lymph nodes and such. I was thrilled as her overall beauty and appearance was not greatly affected. I would have loved her regardless, but I knew that was just one less thing she would have to deal with.

There were some very hard times ahead for her over the next couple of years. What courage it took, to go to work and perform her phone sales position, since it took quite some time before she could talk clearly. She always had to have a glass of water on her desk because of a dry, sore throat, due to radiation and a loss of saliva glands. Those were just the physical battles she faced. She struggled mentally with the possibility of leaving her beautiful 2 year-old daughter motherless. She also had to deal with a naive husband that thought the best thing to do for her was to tell her not to think about it or talk about it, stay positive and everything would be alright. After she had been to a number of counseling sessions to help her emotionally, the doctor wanted to meet with both of us. The doctor asked me how I felt about what both of us had gone through. He also asked how I was helping her to cope with it all. I proceeded to explain how I had been trying to keep her from dwelling on it and that I tried to keep her positive. Those were the most incorrect answers I could have given, and I did it with such proud confidence.

This counselor proceeded to educate me on the damage I had done and explained how uneducated I was in the area of being a supportive spouse. What he said made sense and was a real eye opener to me. By not talking about the situation and simply replying that everything would be alright, she felt that I didn't really care and that it wasn't important enough for me to even talk about it. That could not have been farther from the truth, but that is the message that was projected. I learned that in any crisis a person needs to talk to someone about it. Talking about one's unfortunate situation, regardless of what it is, is a form of therapy. By not talking about it, keeping it all inside, one develops major anxiety and serious consequences can begin to develop. The most natural thing for most people to do, when they experience loss of a friend or family member, a spouse being found to be unfaithful, or when any traumatic situation occurs, is to get on the phone and cover the details with a close friend or maybe with many people. This isn't because they are proud of it, or that they even necessarily want anyone to know, but it is a natural vent and a form of therapy that we are most often naturally driven to engage in.

By not being there for my wife to discuss her feelings with, a barrier began to grow between us and she began to withhold any outward emotion. What an injustice I had dealt her, being the person that should be the most understanding and caring, appearing to not care enough to even talk about her emotional struggles and the threat of a physical reoccurrence of cancer. I had failed big time to be her intimate confidant and ally, independent of what outcome she would experience from the ordeal.

Whether her personality or because of the way I mishandled that whole situation; for years she would not confide in me. There were times I didn't find out about doctor appointments until after they took place. She would frequently find questionable lumps or have symptoms that she would agonize over until a doctor verified everything was all right. The thing I have learned is how important it is to be there for those you are close to. Even if they don't seem to want to talk about a situation, they need to know you are there for them. In a time of someone's crisis, it often feels awkward to appear as prying, so we often choose to say nothing at all. That is most generally interpreted as non-caring. As hard as it may seem, just offer a few words of condolences and they will probably take the opportunity to pour out their heart to you in a much-needed release of information and emotion.

After giving my wife a blessing before surgery, I had a strong belief that everything would be fine. It was such a peace within me that it appeared that I wasn't concerned. That I am sure was easier for me to believe, as it was not my life that hung in the balance. Never the less, I don't feel I had an unfounded comfort. It has been nearly forty years since my wife's surgery and she has not had any reoccurrence of cancer.

That whole ordeal gave me some real perspective to this life. Material things are so minor compared to our health and the well being of our loved ones. Losing a house and the months of toil it took to build, are minor and very forgettable when weighted with the life of a loved one. We are all very mortal, and are granted by and indebted to our Father in Heaven for every breath we take upon this Earth. Regardless of when we think the day of accountability or the second-coming of Christ will take place, if we were suddenly taken from this Earth tomorrow, that day would realistically have arrived. So as we watch someone's life being threatened by a short or long-term illness, there are no guarantees that we will out live them. They simply have some time to prepare and maybe get their life in order; we on the other hand may not. This shouldn't be taken as gloom or hopelessness; but I would only hope to create awareness of the reality each of us face. There is great hope in this life. Regardless of how or when we are called to meet all of those anxiously waiting on the other side of the veil, it should be something that we can look forward to. Although none of us likely feel we are prepared or worthy to stand before God tomorrow, we should have great hope. Regardless of when our time comes it can be a great day for us. Many of the prophets indicated as their lives were being threatened, that it mattered not to them if there lives were spared or not. I believe they had seen or at least been given glimpses of the other side. They also understood the grace available through Christ's atoning sacrifice. With that knowledge, they did not cling to life as tightly as we do, as our limited faith may only offer us uncertainty. If we could get to their level of faith, how much sweeter this life would be, not being shadowed by a fear of dying.

Chapter 8

TWO WITNESSES

After returning to Pocatello it was a short time before we began
trying to put our lives together. Sara returned to work and
eventually that routine aided in making our lives feel a little
reminiscent of our previously normal life. My direction proved
a little harder to rebuild. Construction was slow to recover after
the recession. Trying to edge my way back into a customer
pool I had bowed out of, when leaving for Coeur d Alene, felt
rather strained. The construction world was all I had known
and I had been relatively successful at it; however, I felt very
driven to begin a career doing something that offered more
structure and less volatility. Having sworn I would never waste
my time going to college, proved to leave very few options. So
after weighing the limited paths available to me, I decided to
eat my words and become a student at Idaho State University.

Considering I had been a poor student throughout my entire
life, mathematics being one of my least favorite or successful
subjects, hating the thoughts of a life-long career spent in some
sterile environment, it seemed only logical to enroll in the
Electronics Program. A focused end game caused me to make
the very unlikely decision. My good friend worked for the
Union Pacific Railroad in the Telecommunications Dept. His
job was very diverse and his time was spent in locations
ranging from offices, railroad yards, to mountain tops. He
installed and maintained everything from phones, two way
radios, microwave equipment and any other systems required

to operate a railroad. Every hour spent in the classroom or lab felt like laying pavers on a path to the environment I had envisioned.

Upon graduation there were no jobs available at the Union Pacific. So I began my career at a local Motorola two-way radio shop. It was a great job and provided a foundation that proved very valuable when I began at the railroad fourteen months later.

In order to get a job at Union Pacific I had to relocate to Hermiston, Oregon. Hermiston is in central Oregon and is solely on the map because of the railroad yard, a few miles away. The baron Wyoming type landscape is thirty miles west of the beautiful Blue Mountains near Pendleton and thirty miles east of the scenic Columbia River. My days off were Monday and Tuesday. I was there one year before Sara and our daughter were able to move there.

Working weekends and being separated from my family for a year had not been any part of that initial end game that caused me to choose a career in Electronics. However, a rich blessing came my way as unexpectedly as they always seem to.

I had swapped days off at the request of a fellow employee; which, allowed me to be home during the weekend. I was so excited to have the opportunity to go to church and partake of the Sacrament. I was a little depressed when I found out it was General Conference weekend; which meant no local meetings would be held at the local chapel.

I had never really watched conference before. But that day I decided to watch it and managed to find a channel that aired it. As many often do, I was engaged in some trivial tasks around the house within earshot of the program. Occasionally I would pass by the TV and catch a glimpse of the screen. On one walk-by, I noticed the camera had settled on the Prophet as the Tabernacle Choir began to sing, "We Thank Thee O God For Our Prophet". For some reason it seemed to freeze me in my tracks in front of the TV. I watched as the camera slowly zoomed in on the face of the Prophet. I sat down in the chair as a witness came over me so completely, that it caused my body to melt as tears flowed from my eyes.

Sitting astonished at my reaction, I sat silently wondering if I had created such feelings and then allowed them to run completely out of control. However, those thoughts were cut short, as the very next speaker began. He instructed that we should record the feelings we had received during the previous song. His words removed any doubt that what I had felt was a witness of the Holy Spirit, testifying that a prophet of God sat before my eyes, as the head of the Church of Jesus Christ of Ladder-day Saints.

After marveling that I had been blessed to be part of a miracle, undoubtedly shared with thousands around the world, I gave thanks to God for allowing me to experience that manifestation. It was not because I deserved it, as I so casually watched that conference session. But maybe it was because the Lord knew I needed such strengthening at that time. Although at home that weekend, I had worked weekends for over a year, and it would be another year before I would have the opportunity to go to church.

While recording that wonderful experience in my journal, a realization came over me. If the current president was a true prophet of God, then he had to have received his authority through the succession of prophets since Joseph Smith. And Joseph Smith had to have been given the authority, as he claimed. That one little moment of seeing a prophet of God on TV; and receiving a witness of his authority, gave me a knowledge and assurance; that the current prophet, Joseph Smith, all those between them, and all the prophets of the Book of Mormon were indeed prophets of God. That understanding, like my testimony of the Book of Mormon, was no longer faith, but was suddenly knowledge within me as real as knowing that I had been born of my mother and father. No one could cause doubt of those things by ridicule or throwing false teachings at me.

Having such a firm witness of the divine authority of the Prophets of the Church of Jesus Christ of Latter-day Saints did stir some conflict within me years later. No matter what I studied, learned or knew, I almost cringed when I would see particular pictures of Joseph Smith. I had an unshakable belief in the Book of Mormon and the LDS church. Yet by having such feelings of Joseph Smith, a conflict began to grow within me.

There was a picture of Joseph that showed what appeared to be a shorter, heavy man. Like something Dr. Seuss would say, "I didn't like his looks at all". But it was more than that; it was like that first impression you get of someone when you meet them. There was a gut feeling that he was not a good man. I struggled with that for several years. I would rationalize that you can't decide the character of a man based on the ability of an artist. And an artist's depiction or the physical looks of a person does not have bearing on the soul of a man. But my mind would argue back that I should not have these feelings if he was a good person and a true prophet.

This internal debate caused one of the longest and most extensive searches of anything I have studied. I was determined to end the debate in my mind once and for all. If Joseph was not a prophet of God, then the church could not be true, as he was the one claimed to have received the authority to restore such beliefs and practices. And if he was a true prophet I should not have ill feelings toward him.

In any conflict both sides are going to have bias and see their way as the correct view. But as a judge of any court, you have to weigh the story from each side and determine which one is consistent with the character and facts found separate from the two parties involved. The final element that has to be present, is to be willing to accept the direction that God reveals to you, through prayer, as you make your discoveries and decisions.

I read many things that the opposition uses as proof of Joseph Smith's falsehoods. That being the religion of many, there was no difficulty in finding plenty of material. After reading such things I would try and find the same record within church history and read the other side of the story.

My job at the time caused me to travel throughout the United States. So I had the opportunity to visit many of the places Joseph had lived. I walked and sat at many of the locations that Joseph claimed to have received inspiration and guidance from the Holy Spirit. I stood where he gave the saints direction and charge to do the things that inflamed many at the time. I sat and pondered at the locations where he and his family received persecution that would surely have made me shrink from my cause, be it right or wrong. During those quiet hours spent alone at those locations, and during the hours of isolation in motel rooms recording my findings and feelings, I received a witness.

I received a witness that is greater than all the knowledge I have of the Book of Mormon, of the Prophets, or the Church of Jesus Christ itself. It is knowledge second only to the belief I have of God the Father and Jesus Christ. For, like the knowledge of The Father and The Son, I received a remembrance of the man. Not a remembrance of how he looks, or of any times we may have spent together. But a fondness my heart feels and a reverence my mind generates, to confirm that I knew him very well before coming to this earth. He is a man that is the greatest of all prophets, the one chosen to restore the gospel that Christ himself brought to this earth. He like many freely offered his life as a sacrifice to seal his testimony. In a short time he delivered more information and life saving eternal principles and concepts for the saving of mankind than has any mortal previously or after him. I received a remembrance of a brother and friend that I wished I could have been there to support and buoy up as the darkness tore at him. How I wished I could have sat with him by the river as night approached and let him pour his heart out to me as a brother, and return words of support and praise to strengthen him when those closest to him deserted. What joy it would have brought to sit at his table as a friend and celebrate a child's birthday, with him and Emma after so many tragic losses. That witness and remembrance of the man, brought those feelings alive

51

within my soul. It is warmth as real and dear as the feelings I have of my own brothers. It is knowledge of a man that is as noble as can be found. A man that I would gladly tie my reputation to and would feel so honored if he had reason to mention my name, indicating I helped his cause even in the slightest.

Confirmation from the Spirit is a blessing we are all given as a gift from God. Don't just excuse an idea or information, even if received in a dream. If it seems real, pray about it; pray for understanding if it is unclear and pray for confirmation in all intelligence given to you. God is intelligence and any light or understanding we receive is a gift from God. Praise him and thank him for all that he gives to you

There are so many things I have sought answers to. In each; if I studied, pondered, and prayed; the tiny seed of faith has been replaced with a solid and cherished knowledge. Answers we seek in faith and prayer are often granted, if we seek in wisdom. By wisdom I mean we will not ask for answers our faith will not comprehend or support. If we have wisdom we will not seek answers that we do not need or are irrelevant to our salvation.

Chapter 9

ESCAPING DEPRESSION

This chapter is one of the hardest things I have ever written. There are several contributing factors that made it so difficult. To write about the details of the darkest year of my life, I had to read some of the pages from my journal that I never wanted to revisit. After refreshing my memory with some painful experiences, I then forced my mind to relive those days, trying to capture the deep despair that was a constant companion for that year.

Imagine this book being shown on the big screen in brilliant color cinematography and suddenly the screen changed to a dim, black and white presentation during this chapter. That would almost capture the dramatic change that occurred in my life. It was not gradual, nor was there a small aspect of my life that suddenly became chaotic. Total change occurred overnight and was all consuming.

In 1990 we moved to Portland, Oregon. It was such a promising move and we were so eager to embrace the exciting changes that were on our horizon. However, everything that was good or could have been good or fun, was quickly over-shadowed by so much gloom that it is hard to look back and see anything much that I care to remember.

We were in the middle of a several month process; which involved moving from Pocatello to Salt Lake. My position in Salt Lake suddenly started to look unstable, so we decided to go to Portland instead. We had moved so many times previously, it was not something we were looking forward to.

My wife was pregnant with our third child and was hardly involved in the move. Her submitting a job transfer to Portland was nearly more than she could handle at the time. I had just moved our belongings to Salt Lake, so had to load them all back up and have them shipped to Portland. When I arrived at Portland, I began looking for a home. It was apparent that my wife was overwhelmed at that point, as she did not even want to come help look for a house. The first time she saw our house was when we were moving in. I then realized I must have bought the wrong house. I watched my pregnant wife break out in tears as she wandered from room to room. A coworker helping me, whispered, "That's not a good sign".

Things did improve over the next couple of months. We both settled into our jobs and got our oldest daughter into school and all the recreational activities. My parents lived about forty minutes away from our new home. That was such an anticipated joy of moving to Oregon.

I had worked for my father while growing up. After trying other jobs throughout high school, I returned to work for him just before I got married. Five years later he retired and they moved to Oregon. I really missed being able to spend time around them, after they moved. It was so enjoyable to once again be able to go to their house and watch, as they began to develop relationships with my children.

We had a very wonderful Christmas season with them that year. My mother made such an effort to create a very memorable holiday season for my family and I. We had some great barbeques that year. My dad loved to cook on the grill; which provided entertainment as well as great food. I captured some cherished video footage of my young children with their grand parents and also with my grandmother as she was straying with my parents during that year. Those are precious memories, as my sweet grandmother passed away shortly after that time.

A few months after moving to Portland, I woke up in the middle of the night feeling sick. Within a few hours I told my wife I had appendicitis or a kinked bowel. In an effort to get me to go back to sleep she tried to shame me, for being such a baby about being sick. It was unbelievable to her that I would think the worse, just because I had a slight stomach ache. I stood my ground and indicated that I had such a fine tuned system that I knew when something wasn't right. She threatened to take me to the hospital, again hoping I would just go back to sleep. Instead, I got up and started getting dressed.

Several doctors came throughout the day probing and asking questions. At approximately 5 p.m. another doctor came into my room and began the same routine. He asked if I wanted anything to eat. When I said I would, he made the assumption that I probably didn't have a defective appendix; because most people are sickened by food. He then poked around a little more and I couldn't really pinpoint the pain, just with each previous doctor. He then pushed on my right side and held pressure for about 5 seconds. As he rapidly pulled his hand away, I felt as if he had just ripped my appendix out with his bare hand. I nearly jumped out of bed from the sharp pain. He then chuckled and said, "I'll schedule an operating room for tomorrow morning". I threw a quick victorious smirk in my wife's direction. Her returned grin seemed a little sinister. Thinking about it; I realized my win was about to bring me a lot of pain.

The next morning they performed the operation. It was a very new experience for me. I had always been very blessed with great health and had never had an operation or a broken bone in my life. That was the first of two major surgeries that year and also the one that brought the most change to my life. Following surgery, I was taken to my room with a morphine injection system and an IV attached to my arm. About 9 p.m. they decided to take out the IV, as I would be able to begin eating food the next morning.

When I awoke the following morning, there was something definitely different. Something more than just my plumbing had changed. I felt an eerie presence in the room that was nearly suffocating. It was so disturbing that I could barely force any breakfast into my empty stomach. As I watched TV, I couldn't find a channel that did not seem to intensify the growing gloom around me. I turned off the TV and listened to the radio in an effort to distract my mind; which was so focused on the fear that was building within me. I found that I couldn't stand to listen to any of the radio stations that played my favorite music. The only thing I could begin to tolerate was a classical music station. It wasn't classical rock, but was baroque classical music. That surprised me as much as those that came into my room and would ask what the heck I was listening to. Classical music seemed to be the only thing that could calm me. It wasn't until many years later, through listening to tapes by Michael Balaum that I learned of the actual documented healing powers of classical music.

As each meal came, I ate less and less. By evening I told them I wasn't in much pain so they would remove the morphine pack. I didn't take the pain pills, thinking maybe they had something to do with the horrible realm, in which I had found myself in. I was released the next day and so anticipated the comfort that comes from being at home with family. I was so disappointed to find that the horrible gloomy shadow had followed me from the hospital and now filled the entirety of my home.

After two weeks of eating less and less, and sleeping very little, I went back to work. I was once again hoping that I would snap out of that cycle as I got back to work. I felt that maybe I just had too much time on my hands to think and needed to get back to work. That did not seem to relieve any of the mounting anxiety at all. Work actually started to intensify the insecurity I was beginning to experience.

It became hard to focus on anything at work or home. My mind began to race a hundred miles an hour, day and night. A simple thought or sentence would get stuck in the replay mode, repeating over and over in my mind. On the second day back to work a co-worker and I were to go across town on a trouble call. I asked him to give me a minute while I stepped into the bathroom. I didn't have any need for the facility; but stood silently behind the locked door trying to compose myself. As the words, "I'm OK" endlessly looped in my mind; I tried to calm my breathing while my insides felt like they were vibrating from a fear with no basis. As I rode across town I found it hard to carry on a conversation, even thought my co-worker was an old friend who had been my lab partner during electronics school. My mind tried to juggle the looping, "I'm okay", the frantic reasoning of why this was happening and how could I stop it, and the words coming out of my companion's mouth.

After several weeks I had to return to Salt Lake to help teach an electronics class I had helped to develop before moving to Portland. I nearly canceled but knew I was already obligated to be there. The first day went well, as I felt nearly normal. That night I ate a salad for dinner, but couldn't pass up the free sundae bar. After going to bed at a reasonable time, I woke up about 4 a.m. I was soaking wet and scared to death. That eerie presence was back and stronger than ever. I barely ate breakfast again, due to the terror that was upon me. That day, class was very difficult. I couldn't focus on anything, much less answer questions for students. I am sure most of the students assumed I didn't know what I was teaching because I avoided conversations during lab sessions as much as possible. It was so hard to be polite and cordial or laugh and act like my usual self. Much of the time my throat felt restricted and it was difficult to even swallow. I survived the two weeks at the training facility, yet felt I had really performed poorly.

At work or at home, the minutes became like hours and hours like days. I began to have night terrors; waking up soaking wet and feeling as though something terrible had happened. Daytime wasn't much better. I felt nauseated much of the time, whether from diet or fear I'm not sure. One evening after work, I went out to mow the lawn; anything to avoid sitting idle and having time to think. As I mowed I became faint and broke out in a sweat. My vision became very dim, as if I was trying to look through a tiny peephole. As bad as it may sound, that was the first glimpse of joy I had experienced since the surgery. That was a familiar symptom I could relate to, having experienced it previously in my life. It was the same symptom I had felt in Junior High the first time I experienced a reaction to having a low blood sugar level.

I went into the house and ate something immediately. The distortion and weakness disappeared. That was very confusing to me. I had had minor symptoms of low blood sugar all my adult life, but had never experienced any of the new developments. I immediately started trying to find a doctor that could treat me. The first Doctor I went to needed a lot of development in his bed side approach. I mentioned that I had already controlled the dizziness and related symptoms through diet, but was still battling all the sleeplessness, nausea, and anxiety of hypoglycemia, to which he just shook his head. At that point he proceeded to tell me there was no such thing

I left his office embarrassed and even more depressed. I had confided in a doctor, which took enormous courage, only to be told I was nearly crazy. That made it very hard to find enough confidence to call another doctor. While looking through the yellow pages, I found the actual word hypoglycemia listed under the diabetic center. As I called and explained my symptoms, they scheduled me to meet with a doctor.

When I went to the clinic, I was still experiencing very scary nights and long dreary days. I went into the wrong entrance when I arrived at the clinic. Entering the pharmacy by mistake, I waited for the people in front of me to finish, so I could ask for directions. The lady told them she was there to pick up a prescription for lithium. It was obvious which one was the patient. I assume the thirty year old standing slightly behind her was her son. His clothing looked as though he had quickly dressed himself from the hamper, and he hadn't made it to the bathroom to brush his hair. As he quickly glanced back at me I saw the same lost, fearful look in his eyes that were reflected in my mirror that morning. When his mother turned around to leave, I could see that his demanding care had drained the life from her body. For a moment I could picture myself getting one notch worse and being in his shoes; causing the life to be drained from my wife as she took me to my appointments and cared for me.

Meeting with the doctor that afternoon gave me a glimmer of hope. He indicated that the symptoms I had been experiencing were symptoms associated with hypoglycemia. The times that I skipped meals due to anxiety only increased the symptoms, because my blood sugar would slip even lower. Going to bed without eating a snack, or eating anything with sugar before bed, could cause severe night terrors. He went on to inform me, that unlike diabetes that can be controlled with medication, hypoglycemia can only be controlled by diet. He did educate me on what were the correct things to eat and the time frame to eat them in. Prior to that I felt I had already cut out the sugar from my diet, but was wrong. The Gatorade I had been living on was mostly glucose, a form of sugar, the same thing found in an IV. He helped me to understand that the surgery had probably triggered the condition. It could have been that being on an IV all day, stopping it at 9 p.m. and not eating until the next morning had jolted my pancreas into that mode of operation. Or a trauma such as surgery itself can sometimes bring on diabetes or hypoglycemia.

That was novel, a doctor that agreed that a pancreas could be too active or inactive just as a thyroid that swings in both directions, or blood pressure that can go either direction. If you ever encounter such symptoms and a doctor refuses to discuss the possibilities of diabetes or hypoglycemia, find a new doctor.

For many months I read and studied anything I cold find on diet and eating correctly. The symptoms lessened some but were still sever. I had lost 30 pounds and had dark rings under my eyes. The nights I didn't wake up in terror, I woke up afraid I wouldn't be able to sleep. The minute I opened my eyes in the morning, I could feel if the gloom was present or not. If I woke up and could feel it, it was there all day usually. I could experience it 1-6 days in a row and then maybe have a somewhat normal day or two. There didn't seem to be any pattern or way to predict it. I also had severe headaches the majority of the days.

My third daughter was about to be born. The births of my previous two daughters were something I had been present for and had enjoyed as very special experiences. The delivery was planned and scheduled as a sycerien delivery. They took my wife into the operating room to prep her and begin as I got dressed in scrubs. Approaching the operating rooms, there were two doctors scrubbing up. One commented how he couldn't believe that they had lost her. Assuming they were not talking about my wife, I looked through the windows until I found the room she was in. Walking in, I sat down at her head. She was out like a light, which really surprised me. They had indicated that she would only receive an epidural but not a general anesthetic. Then I started recalling the discussion I had heard in the hallway. No one in the room greeted me nor was even talking amongst themselves. I began watching my wife's face very closely, trying to see if I could see her breathing. After what seemed to be an eternity, the anesthesiologist leaned over and told me he had to knock her out because she was freaking out. After I noticed shallow breathing, I felt a little better, but remained suspicious.

They told me they were ready to deliver the baby, so I should stand up to watch. The baby wouldn't come out so the doctor ended up with his arms up to his elbows inside of my wife's stomach cavity. When he still couldn't get the baby out, the doctor switched the nurse places. He then proceeded to push and pound on her stomach. Eventually he reached up inside and cut some scar tissue from a previous delivery and then the baby came out. I sat down twice to regroup during the ordeal. It was like being forced to watch the goriest horror show ever.

As gloom or terror was nearly a constant companion I poured out my heart continually to God, begging for some kind of relief. I began wondering if my condition was dietary, mental, or something evil. Shortly after the episode at the hospital I became sensitized to the color red. I don't know if it was from seeing the most gruesome blood bath imaginable, but I could not stand the color red. If I was walking and caught a glimpse of something red out of the corner of my eye, my reflexes would cause me to jump as though a snake had just struck at me. It wasn't as if I disliked anything red, I absolutely couldn't tolerate it. Violence on TV became so intensive. There did not seem to be anything on TV that did not include violence or corruption of some manner. I feared that I would wake up and something would have happened to my family by my hand or someone else's. I knew that I was not capable of harming my family, but wondered if I was developing schizophrenia or something.

My family loved to watch unsolved mysteries. I couldn't stand to watch it because there seemed to be a lot of people that appeared very normal and then just came up missing, or that all of the sudden went on a killing spree. I was terrified that I would wake up some day to find I had done something of that manner. However, in most of the cases on TV, they would almost always find that those types of people had been plotting for some time, enabling them to collect money or be with a lover. That gave me some comfort, as I knew I had none of that action going on.

My wife and I drove to and from work together often. Prior to developing that condition, I had loved the opportunity of riding together. Now; however, it had become almost more than I could do. The drive normally took 30 to 40 minutes. My mind could be racing through thought after thought and yet I may only get 1 or 2 sentences out of my mouth the entire drive. I was so afraid I was going crazy and knew that I acted very different. My wife would often comment and ask what was wrong. Just that simple question took an eternity to reply, "Nothing". I would stare at her wondering if I should tell her how bad it had gotten, but was afraid I would scare her. Then she would get nervous and ask why I was starring at her.

My normal driving route to drop off and pick up my wife took me through downtown Portland. There were several places that homeless people lined the streets. It became totally unbearable to drive through those areas. I tried to find alternate routes to avoid seeing those desperate people. The reason it bothered me so, was that I could see myself amongst them. I knew that if I progressively got any worse, I would not be able to function within society and could not bear to have my wife and children burdened or to see me that way. Therefore, I would have to disappear into the ranks of the homeless, who a large number of them are there due to a mental condition.

Each day it became harder to drive across the bridge that allowed me to get to my office. It was so tempting to just cause a wreck by jerking the steering wheel; which would result in me going off the bridge to a guaranteed death. That way my family would be able to grieve, thinking it was an accident and not put any blame or embarrassment on themselves.

During the year we lived in Portland my grandmother passed away, as well as one of my very good friends. I was not able to return to Pocatello to attend either funeral due to work and finances. That is something I have regretted for a long time. For months after the funerals, I would think of how lucky both of them were, to have died and have escaped this life.

After being in Portland for approximately seven months, I was offered a promotion; which would return us to Salt Lake after a few additional months. I had to think long and hard before accepting. A promotion would make me more visible and could be more stressful. I just wasn't sure I could handle either at that time. So I spent a lot of hours asking God what to do, knowing that either moving or staying in Portland would require God's help for me to be successful. I accepted the position having faith that God would help me and knowing that I couldn't let this condition prevent me from securing a better future for my family.

The new job required a considerable amount of travel. Every time I got on a plane I hoped it would go down. It removed any anxiety of flying, but I sure hope I never get someone like that on one of my flights now.

It was about that time that I found some very good books on hypoglycemia. I read about case after case of people suffering from very similar situations. One of them was a famous talk show host. He had to give up his show because he could not concentrate or put two sentences together. He, as well as many others recovered to a normal life with a controlled diet. I talked to my cousin that had battled the disease for years in search of some answers. Through education and diet I began to again care for life and cope with a lot of my problems. I could see that there might be a day that I may gain my life back.

My parents had a neighbor that was having a battle with life, which seemed very similar to what I was experiencing. While I was talking to my father, he indicated that the man had threatened suicide. He had said that the doctor could not find anything wrong with him and had him on some medication. Being concerned for this individual, my father asked if I would talk to him. Just prior to moving from Portland I spent a long time on the phone with this poor man one night. We discussed the common feelings we were both experiencing. I went into great detail as to what dietary changes he should make, just to see if he could find some relief. After going to the doctor the following week and explaining what I had discussed with him, he was told to forget it all. The doctor convinced him that diet had nothing to do with it. I know that every case is different, but I fail to see what harm a healthy diet would have on someone, even if it were not a cure. I know the hopeless fear he must have felt as he left that doctor's office, thinking a cure was not obtainable. He left behind his wife and child the following week after taking his own life. The news jolted me back to wondering if I would ever really be free of the fear that swallowed up that poor soul.

We moved to Salt Lake one year from when we arrived in Portland. I called a doctor at the diabetic center when I arrived in Salt Lake. I guess I was hoping she had a new cure for those sever mood swings I still experienced. She told me I would have to go through a General Practitioner and be referred to her. As I met with the General Practitioner, he told me he felt I was battling chemical depression. He explained that there are two kinds of depression. Traumatic things that happen can bring on one type of depression. The other type is caused by a chemical imbalance. The symptoms for hypoglycemia and depression are almost identical. I agreed to try some medication, as I did not feel I had anything to lose.

Medication for depression comes in several forms. I had heard so much bad press about Prosaic, that I was reluctant to use it. He prescribed Pamolar, a milder drug with the reports of few if any side effects. The only side effect that I experienced was drowsiness initially; which diminished with time. As explained to me, the drug is similar to vitamins, in that the body uses what it needs and sloughs off the rest. Each appointment the doctor would read down the list of symptoms he recorded during our first visit. He slowly increased the dosage of Pamolar and would check each time to see which symptoms still existed. After several months I realized most of the symptoms had disappeared. I could hardly remember feeling most of the horrible things of the past. He then maintained that level for months before beginning to taper off the dosage, still checking on symptoms each appointment. Suddenly some symptoms began to reoccur so he increased the dosage slightly and we maintained that level of dosage for nine months. I then went off the medication and my body seemed to have been jump started and didn't require the medication any longer. I credit that doctor with saving my life. I was so sad when years later he had to take an early medical retirement and I was forced to find a new doctor.

Even when all the symptoms of depression and anxiety were in check due to the medication, I still experienced distorted vision, sweating, weakness, and some nausea. Those seemed to be somewhat controlled and affected by diet. Therefore, I am not sure if my problems were all depression or a combination of depression and hypoglycemia. All I know is that I am so thankful that I ran into that particular doctor, at that particular time.

As I look back on that time now, it seems like a dream or someone else's life. While in that condition or state of mind; it seemed so real and that there could never be a bright day again. The only thing that kept me from taking my life was the belief that it would be considered as murder in the eyes of the Lord. I know that the Lord and only He, has the right to determine when we have completed all He has sent us here to experience. Had my state of mind gotten any worse, I am not sure I would have been rational enough to think that clearly or even care. In that case I would hope that the mercy of the Lord would determine what was right and wrong.

At various times of my life, I have experienced righteous highs and lows. Some of the real lows were as I was trying to return to the graces of God. I have felt the adversary as if he was sitting next to me, at times so strong that I turned back away from prayer and repentance out of fear. I know that brought great joy and victory to Satan. That was eventually overcome by prayer, which restored light and joy into my life.

I had taken drugs earlier in my life, which caused me to experience the same fear and feeling of gloom and hopelessness. That disappeared as the effect of the drugs wore off. I guess that was what was most disturbing about the two years that I battled that emotional rollercoaster. There did not seem to be any feeling of relief or hope. I could not seem to find any comfort through prayer or reasoning. There were times that I prayed nearly all day and all night long, looking for some comfort or peace to come into my heart. I wondered if religion or even God was real. I started questioning whether I understood anything about this life or our existence. There were days that I rationalized, maybe I was possessed and needed to have demons cast from me. It seemed at times, that maybe I was just going prematurely senile. I felt like those you see while walking through a nursing home; people terrified and hiding from unseen things and unexplained feelings of fear.

I do not know whether this was forced upon me to give me some sort of insight, or if it just happened. Whatever the reason, I did gain a changed perspective of myself and those around me. Each day as I awake, I know it is a blessing to be able to successfully accomplish tasks, to have a clear mind and a calm heart. I found mental instability to be so much more devastating than any physical battles I have ever encountered. I enjoy lying in bed or relaxing and being able to ponder the good things in my life, without being consumed with an artificial fear that prevents me from sitting still. It is a pleasure to hold my wife and children, knowing I am not capable of harming them, but instead, someone that can protect and provide for them, that hopefully they respect and look up to. My heart feels great sorrow and is touched as I see homeless or mentally ill people. And I have a great faith and knowledge that the Lord does hear and answers my prayers. I feel so blessed, as I am often embraced by His Spirit, touching and strengthening me in ways I can't even describe.

Chapter 10

FAR WEST

I attended a Business meeting in Kansas City during the year of 2001. The meeting had no importance to me; because I felt that I was not going to be working with the company much longer. However, I was still very excited to go because several of my coworkers are members of the LDS church and are always interested in taking in any historic sites and engaging in some interesting theological discussions. Having been to the area several times, I was anxious to share my perspective with them about Independence and Far West.

One afternoon as we had some free time, my friend Paul and I went to the LDS visitors center at Independence, MO.(part of Kansas City). The enjoyable three hours passed so quickly.

The next afternoon following another day of meetings, we again had some time to go do what we wanted. Paul and two others were interested in seeing Far West and Adam-ondi-Ahmen. There were also two other individuals that didn't have anything to do; they too wanted to go along. The additional two were not members of the LDS faith so the focus of the discussions ended up being a little different than we had expected. However, it was enjoyable to share the rich history of the area and provide an overview of our beliefs with them.

During the several hour trip, it was surprisingly delightful to have everyone interested and engaged in various perspectives of faith. One was quite involved in his church and the other was not religious at all. The dynamics caused the discussions to spread across the horizon.

We made it to Adam-ondi-Ahman without much effort. After spending some time there we intended to find Far West on our way back. We missed it somehow and after overshooting it, we were back in Kansas City before we knew it. Rather than backtracking, the group decided they were ready for dinner. That was a disappointment for a couple of us, as we were to leave the next day.

After our meeting the following day, Paul and I were headed to the airport together to return the rental car and catch our flights. While headed to get some lunch Paul expressed real disappointment that we hadn't made it to Far West. Deciding we had enough time to go there and still catch our flights, we got our lunch to go and ate on the way to Far West.

It was a rainy day and the rental car was super small, I'm sure it was barely legal to be on the freeway. Heading north out of Kansas City, the storm became very violent, with strong winds and heavy rain. I could barely keep the car on the freeway and had to reduce our speed to about 30 miles per hour. After turning off the freeway it became even more severe, as we traveled on the narrow country road. I then reduced my speed to 20 miles per hour; because my wipers could not keep up with the severe torrential rain. Helplessly sitting in the passenger seat, Paul suggested that maybe we shouldn't go any farther. Feeling a little more in control with the wheel in my hands, my reasoning that we were nearly there, kept us moving forward. I began praying silently because I really wanted him to see it and felt it was important to him. He taught Sunday School classes on church history each week and really wanted to be able to teach them of that area with first hand knowledge. So my prayer wasn't for me to see it, because I had been there several times; but it was because of my desire for him to see it.

There were several places that the flood water was washing down the hills, burying the highway under the rich brown soil from the planted fields. Again Paul said maybe we should turn back. By then we were just coming up on our destination, to our great relief. It was raining so hard that I could barely see the building across the road from the Far West temple plot. Not being able to read the sign because of the rain, I wasn't able to satisfy Paul's curiosity, of whether it was part of the Church's property.

As I began turning into the parking lot, my wipers were still not able to keep up with the rain. Just as I pulled into the lot of Far West, the rain stopped immediately. Astonished, Paul asked if the rain had actually stopped and I replied that I thought we had just pulled under the trees. I offered Paul my jacket; because I knew he wouldn't have time to change clothes when we got to the airport. Having a little later flight, I was sure I would have time to change my clothes if they were wet. We then exited the car, intending to get soaked the minute we stepped from under the trees.

To our surprise there were no trees directly over our head and yet not a drop of water was falling on us. We just sort of grinned at each other because we knew it was really unbelievable as we could see the heavy rain still falling in the road twenty yards away.

We moved quickly because we knew we didn't have much time and felt the rain would probably begin falling very soon. As we stepped from the concrete stairs onto the grass that filled the area within the temple corner stones, we sank into water that was standing on the saturated ground. We walked to read the informative plaques near each of the cornerstones. We stood and admired the beautiful granite slabs that offered a brief history of the church and those sacred temple grounds.

I mentioned to Paul that the water was right to the tops of my shoes and was amazed at how much water had fallen during the storm. I have walked on sidewalks with water barely standing on them and have not been able to keep the water out of dress shoes. So I knew I was going to be wet the way we were briskly walking through the grass.

We returned to the car after about ten minutes and Paul got in to drive. As he pulled to the road he began to turn right. I stopped him and told him we needed to go left. He was under the impression the sign up the road identified more items to see. It was a sign indicating how far it was to Adam-ondi-Ahman; however. He expressed that he wanted to spend a little more time at Far West then; the control clearly now in his hands. He backed the car into the lot and we exited the car, still not a drop of rain falling on us.

We walked around the grounds and up the hill. As I stood on the hill adjacent to the temple plot, the view provided an interesting perspective. Temple locations are usually set on a hill to gain advantage of the surrounding terrain, allowing them to be seen from considerable distances. This location was no different. Even though the terrain had less elevation changes than are present in the west, it was still the location that could be seen for great distances above the rolling terrain. The site is still dedicated for a temple and will someday see a temple build on that portion of ground. At that time, it will be a beacon on the hill.

It was a little scary as we stood on that bare high point of ground; the sky rumbling with thunder, as lightning stabbed the ground in every direction around us. I somehow didn't feel threatened though. We stood up a young tree that had recently been planted. The rain and winds of the storm had bent it completely over so the root ball was out of the ground. I realized I hadn't taken any pictures yet, so I retrieved the camera out of the car and began taking pictures as quickly as I could. Again I was walking through the grass very quickly to get pictures. I took a picture of the water half way up on my shoes; the outside leather quite wet.

We returned to the car after spending a total of about 20-30 minutes there. After getting in the car we compared notes; our hair, shirts and socks were not wet in the least. Turning left I pulled the car onto the road and it was as if we had pulled into a car wash. Immediately the wipers could not keep up with the water. We both started laughing with astonishment. It was something I knew people would not believe if they were not there. Our laughter was because we knew we had witnessed something that was totally unbelievable and unexplainable, yet we had both experienced it so it was very real.

It turned out we had plenty of time when we got to the airport. The severe storm covered the entire area and for several hours planes were diverted and not allowed to land. I comfortably sat in the airport with dry cloths and thoughts of all that we had experienced.

I was mystified over why such an unbelievable thing had happened. I considered it a miracle. Not because it was earth shattering or of a large magnitude; but because it was so obvious that situation could not have naturally happened. There had to be some type of intervention to prevent rain from falling on a one-block area in the midst of driving rain, winds, lightning and thunder. I didn't feel the wind blowing while we were there, yet I could barely keep the car on the road going there and returning to the airport. How can wind be blowing a storm through, yet you don't feel it as you stand amid grass and trees bending, under the severe conditions? I learned that miracles are not only provided when dire emergencies beg their occurrence. Miracles can happen for our mere convenience or for a person's testimony to be strengthened in some way. It also confirmed the validity that God can certainly control the elements of this earth; possessing the ability to have provided the miraculous creation that he has blessed us with.

I don't know if the intervention was for my benefit or for Paul's. Maybe it was for both of our benefit. I know Paul was appreciative he was able to see those things and my prayer was answered for him. The experience gave me just another reason why I can't deny the power and existence of God, the power of prayer, and His awareness of our lives, even to the smallest degree. I have been shown that our prayers are listened to and answered even when they are for non-life threatening things.

Chapter 11

THE DREAM

Anyone that has experienced marriage beyond the honeymoon, has undoubtedly experienced a rough patch or two. Those unpleasant times ripple through our lives, ranging from just not talking as often as we should, to arguing for hours. Some people get it out of their system quickly, while others drag it out for days. First they may talk too much and then follow it up with days of silence toward each other.

Every couple seems to have their own style, as unique as fingerprints. There is the real challenge to making any marriage work. Every relationship is different; therefore, no one set of successful rules, instruction book, or experiences, will necessarily be the key for the next situation. It becomes a challenge for both parties in the relationship to work together; being willing to give and take until they find that magic middle ground, where they can both exist happily with one another.

If a couple doesn't find that middle ground, and one party is forced to do all the compromising, the partnership will eventually run into trouble. A person in love may be willing to do all the bending for some time; however, will likely resent it eventually. When an individual gets to that point, they may become totally inflexible or worse yet, just lose total respect and compassion for their mate. If the relationship evolves to that stage, they will often want to end the relationship and have no desire to try and work it out. Many times, as people lose the respect and compassion for their mate, as if by fate, their perfect soul mate suddenly crosses their path. Often they too are frustrated with a relationship, the result seem to follow a very predictable path.

First, there is infatuation with the new person in their life. As the feelings grow, they become more frustrated with their existing relationship, causing greater resentment with each minor confrontation. Next they begin to realize how they may have let their physical appearance deteriorate over the years; while they were content and not feeling a need to impress their current partner. So they shed that unwanted weight and change a few of their annoying and less attractive habits. That continues until, not only the mate, but friends begin to notice the changes. As anyone inquires, it is blown off as depression, job, or stress.

As treatment for each other worsens, the historically overbearing party becomes very passive and willing to try anything to make it work. However, the newly found freedom and self-esteem makes "the beaten down" unwilling to change. No longer having any desire to work at the old relationship; they determine they have not been happy for a long time. In fact, they are not sure they have ever known love. A short time latter they bitterly part their ways. After swearing over and over, that there isn't anyone else, they miraculously are remarried within four to six months. Not all failed relationships follow this path. However, like me, you have probably watched too many friends or family members go through this very painful pattern of events. It does not seem to be gender specific, as either party may find themselves in one role or the other.

The scriptures instruct to never betray your spouse in word, thought, or deed. What great words of direction. Those few words can be boiled down to respect. That one very simple concept can be the saving grace of any relationship and yet the lack of, nearly guarantees failure.

The first time I saw my wife, I was a junior in high school. It was one of those total-consuming things that turned my life upside down. From that very moment nothing else mattered to me. All my energy was expelled in trying to make her a part of my life. I rerouted my path to classes just to up the odds of being able to say hello as she passed by. A tardy was a small price to pay. When she became willing to say more than just hello, I would even take an absence from my next class, if it meant getting the chance to talk to her.

Then came the classical setback: as I tirelessly worked toward getting a date, she was trying to arrange for her friend and I to go out. How could I have been so misread? Eventually, we got that straightened out and we began dating. We dated off and on for several years. Even when we were broke-up, I was so concerned about her. I was so worried about what she was doing or who she was with. That was very unusual for me. Prior to that, I had never been so completely occupied by anyone.

We dated for years and eventually got married. Our first five years of marriage were so carefree and enjoyable. I would choose to change nothing. Once you have children, you cannot come home on Friday at 5 o'clock and decide to take off for the weekend, be on the road by 5:30, and return Sunday night. Those years remain irreplaceable in my eyes. We enjoyed each other and did everything together. Not only were we married to each other, but we were also each other's best friend. To this day, I have not found a better friend. I have confided things to her that I would not feel comfortable telling another soul.

Next came the years of children. That really adds another dimension to your world. It is a love that is different than spousal love, but every bit as special and rewarding. But with children, comes a complexity and strain on any marriage. It can be a challenge for a sound marriage, and disastrous to one based solely on physical attraction or money.

Like other couples, we too had our times of struggle that varied in severity. Shortly after passing that twenty fifth year milestone, we hit one of those rough patches; at least I seemed to. We were not having major disagreements over any issues. We didn't seem to even be outwardly fighting. I just did not feel there was much happening between us, good or bad. After going to bed one night, I lay in the silence that seemed to engulf our bedroom. Thoughts of what a relationship should be like, after twenty five years, swirled around in my mind. Each time a sentence threatened to escape my mouth and provoke a discussion, pride pushed it back down my throat. Those retreating words tasted bitter and filled me with more unfounded resentment. Wearying of such exhausting battles, I wondered if she was even aware of the conflict, while lying in the same bed. The deafening internal debate continued. "Shouldn't there be more to a relationship after all these years?" the question offered anonymously. My internal voice rationalizing, "maybe relationships can't sustain those wonderful feelings for each other, year after year. The discontented debate continued as I drifted off to sleep.

That night I had a very stirring dream. It was very simple, yet had profound effects. I am very aware of who was anonymously providing my mind with all the fuel to stoke the anger and discontent during those dark days. However, I also know without a doubt, where the essence of that dream came from; which was so simple, with very little dialogue, yet able to shock the very foundation of my soul. It was from the only Entity that knows the disabling feelings I experienced the very first time I saw my wife's face.

The dream began with me simply gazing upon my wife's face. It wasn't a recollection of any particular event or time in our lives that I could recall; that was evident not to be the focus. I saw my wife, just as she was when we were in high school. It wasn't just a glance, or a passing thing. We were very close to one another, yet not touching or speaking. There were no distractions, sounds or noticeable background. We were simply looking into each other's eyes for a brief moment of time. Her

76

radiant blue eyes, soft smile, and golden hair took me directly to the days of our early courtship. There was not a line on her face or a trace of the weight the previous years had generously provided each of us. While looking deeply into her eyes, as she did the same, all those initial feelings were rekindled. All those extreme feelings that make your voice suddenly operate a couple octaves higher and remove the air from your lungs, preventing you from completing a sentence in a single breath. I felt the weakness that sweeps over you, leaving you wondering if you are going to be able to remain standing. It was the consuming force that makes you skip classes, being willing to suffer any consequence just to have a few more moments together.

As indicated, nothing was said; we did not embrace, or even touch each other. But the feelings of love and compassion were overwhelming. That renewed image was burned into my heart and the intense feelings of love remained even after I awoke. Joy and appreciation burst within me as she lay sleeping next to me. I no longer saw the person from the night before and the dissenting voice could find no place in the room.

As those we love mature and age, it is easy to lose track of who they are. I could suddenly see beyond the changes demanded by time, and see the person that stirred such incredible emotion in me years ago. How lucky I was to be next to the one that knew me better than anyone in the world, and that I had shared so much of my life with. Her beauty and character that drove me crazy years ago, was all right there next to me.

That dream was very different from your normal dream. I know everyone has dreams that cause disappointment as they wake up. Even if feelings or events seem so real, by that evening you have pretty much forgotten them. You may even go to sleep hoping the dream continues where it left off, but it never does. That is why my dream was so different. When I woke up, I did not regret that the dream was over. In fact, I was thrilled I was awake, and could enjoy seeing my wife for real. The dream or its effects have not escaped me. Maybe the feelings are not as strong as when I initially awoke. But there is always that reminder present; which causes me to look beyond that ever familiar face. Her beauty and joy has always made her the only person I would want to be with for eternity.

Chapter 12

A MOTHER'S UNDERSTANDING

My mother called me one evening to tell me that my Aunt was just diagnosed as terminal and they had given her about three weeks to live. She was the wife of my mother's brother. Her cancer of a few years previous had returned. My mother asked me if I could send her a card or something. Our family had reservations to have a family reunion in Lincoln City, Oregon a few weeks later so her fear was that none of us would be able to go to the funeral. My mother and father were planning to see her the following week.

My wife and our youngest daughter were in Europe for a couple of weeks. Sara had signed them up for a tour through the school, which was a great program. She felt Amy graduating that year, meant it would be the last time they would be able to take advantage of the program.

With Sara gone, I decided I would drive to Emmett and visit my dying Aunt Dorothy. My oldest daughter, Erin, was in Bear Lake for the 4th of July weekend and my middle daughter, Emily, was going to hang out with her friends. She offered to go with me because she is so kind; but, she didn't know my Aunt, so I told her she didn't need to go. Besides, I expected the 11 hours of solitude, while driving, would surely shape my perspective of the solemn feelings that were growing within me.

I had made the trip from Pocatello to Boise countless times during my life. I believed it to be at the top of the list of the most painful drives in the U.S. That was before I had ever made the trip from Salt Lake to Boise, via Snowville.

Continuing from the Tremonton Junction toward Snowville, the beauty began. The view of monochrome grass and sagebrush expanded across the horizon, would not change for the next several hours. The sparse traffic and straight-line highway encouraged some multi-tasking, so I began listening to a recorded talk by Cleon Skowsen.

By listening to the inspirational talk and my mind drifting between prayer and pondering various things in my life, I began to have a flow of thoughts that were undeniably not my own. I have learned to recognize that as, the Spirit teaching me. It came in waves with tears randomly filling my eyes. It was such an awesome experience and I am so blessed to have such a gift, as I know it to truly be a gift.

I had tried a couple of times to focus on the design and fabrication of something I was developing; however I could not concentrate for some reason. So I returned to thinking about my aunt and whether to give her one of my books I had brought with me. The book referenced the importance of families, repentance and our Savior. The last section is a collection of poems and thoughts about returning home after we die. I have seen it bring people peace when they are ready to die; but I was concerned it would offend her or her family. There are references to LDS beliefs in many of the stories and poems; which may have caused her or her family to feel I was trying a last-ditch effort to convert her to the LDS faith. So I thought and thought about whether I should give it to her. During the debate I began to think about how happy my mother would be if my Aunt could find that she and my mother believed in the same Jesus Christ. My mother's parents, brothers and sisters have all questioned her joining the church after she married my father. My Aunt and her children were active in their church and I am sure they always heard, like many religions teach, how wrong the LDS faith is.

All my life I have known my mother was the only one in her family that accepted the LDS faith. She has been so good to them and is a great example of her faith; however they never inquired about her beliefs in the least. I am sure they all talked behind her back, about how much she has given up for her church; especially, after her and my dad went on a mission. Having that knowledge of her situation I never made even the slightest connection between her and me. I have thought briefly at times that it must be hard on her to feel like she was on the outside of her family, even though she did everything to be close to them. But my thoughts and concerns were so shallow.

As I drove to Emmett, my understanding of her pain changed so dramatically. Cleon Skowsen's talk about the Atonement and the scriptures played in the background, as my thoughts were of my Aunt. I thought about her passing and how happy she will be when she again sees her parents and brothers and sisters. She will also be so pleased to see that my mother had found the joy of the gospel while on earth. I believe she will have disappointment, that she did not reach out to my mother and find out about her beliefs. Because, she could have also had so much more understanding here on earth, had she done so. She is a wonderful and religiously committed person so I don't think she will have any regrets about how she lived. She will undoubtedly accept God and his plan. But to know she could have enjoyed greater things here if she would have just listened or talked to my mother, will weigh on her.

It was in such thought that my eyes were opened up to see my mother in a new dimension. She often tells me it must be hard to keep going to church when my family does not go and I am there alone. I tell her it is ok and inside appreciate her recognition. But at the same time I have never realized she speaks about it from first-hand knowledge. I have not made the link before; because her husband and children are in the church. But I know the bonds between our parents and siblings are as strong and as important as those of our spouse and offspring. They are different but they are as important and as meaningful. Just like the love for our spouse and our children, or the love of one child over another is different, they are all equally important. I began to feel the pain my mother must have felt for so many years as she had seen one family member after another pass. She watched them pass, while remaining unsuccessful at sharing the gift of the gospel with them. She was an example of a true saint, year after year, demonstrating what true sacrifice for God looks like.

I realized my mother had often consoled me, as if needed, for having gone to church alone for so many years. Her compassion created through eyes of true understanding. She had prayed and sought for a solution for me even though she continued to walk the same path herself.

I have been blessed with so many spiritual experiences that have sustained me throughout my life. I once had a sweet little lady tell me of her situation that was exactly as mine, from the perspective of the non-member wife. She told me, my responsibility was to endure even unto death and to let God be the guardian of my wife. My Patriarchal Blessing also tells me to endure to the end and never betray my wife. Clearly God needed to impress upon me how valuable she is to Him. Having a view of my future, my weaknesses and my needs, God placed a path of endurance before me, meant to develop strength and provide an avenue for blessings.

My mother had endured even longer with no such encouragements and experiences. She told me years ago she had never really felt the Spirit. I do not even come close to the stature of my mother. She has been such an example to all of her family; being a portrayal of true faith. I have needed continual boosting from God to continue. I suddenly fully appreciated her pain rather than considering mine. I began sobbing as you do when the Spirit teaches you. Then it was as if I could hear the Spirit say, "Now you see". My ears suddenly began to hear the talk on the stereo. It was as if it had just been turned on. Although it had been playing the whole time, I had been so deep in thought I had not been listening to it.

The words playing on the stereo right then:

"Every once in awhile you will begin to cry. Those tears mean that God is talking to you. You wonder why you are crying when you feel so good. Kneel down immediately and thank God for talking to you."

I began to laugh through the tears.

1. Because I did feel so good having been taught of my mother's understanding of my situation; causing me to feel less alone.
2. Because I found it so humorous that those precise words played just at that moment. I truly love God for his compassion, concern, and his sense of humor.

It is hard to explain to anyone why there is pain when you see people that do not accept the gospel. It doesn't mean they are a bad person in any manner. They may be a far better person than many people that belong to the LDS faith. But the blessings of the gospel are such a wonderful gift to have on this earth. To just have the Spirit talk to you one time is indescribable. The gospel offers a source of knowledge and guidance from current Prophets; which, I know are providing a road map through the hardest and darkest times in the earth's history. Modern day Prophets are directing the preparations taking place to prepare for Christ to return and claim his reign of this world. It is such a blessing to have clear doctrine, when so many feel they have been left here in darkness, with no answers, just waiting to see what happens. How hard would that be?

To have joy swell within you, to have love for someone you really don't know, to have understanding of someone's problems when you don't really know how you know of their situation, are all gifts of the Holy Ghost. Living according to the higher law that Christ provided during his earthly mission, entitles that person the constant companionship of the Holy Ghost. To have the authority to protect your family with the priesthood power that God used to create the universe, is a true blessing; which you wished everyone could have. It is Christ's pure love that causes people to share the gospel. It is not a belief that someone is not a good person because they are not a member. But it is the greatest gift on this earth that you know will bring overall and fully encompassing joy to every person that possesses it. So if you find joy in helping a stranger or even a friend find this true happiness, what greater joy would it bring you to see the ones you love the most on this earth, embrace the gospel of peace and joy?

Chapter 13

DEJA VU

I had fasted and prayed numerous times throughout the month, while trying to get some inspiration, as to what I should do with my fabrication business. I had been debating whether or not to close the doors, due to losing money for nearly six months. Being behind on my house mortgage, I didn't see that being resolved any time soon either. My concern also included that I had worked two years building our house as well as a spec house. My goal was to use money from the sale of the houses, to push the fabrication business through the slow period we had been experiencing. I had hoped it would create some needed cash for inventory, paying down bills, and to get ahead of delinquent taxes. However, it didn't seem to be working, as neither house would sell due to a sluggish housing market.

We had put our retirement money into Retro in hopes of investing in ourselves. I know I had God's help to make Retro work for years. I started a business from scratch and saw miracles happen routinely to keep us growing against the odds. We were doing something that had not been done before. Utah being home to a large percentage of entrepreneurs, many people tried to copy our business model. But we had always managed to remain a couple steps ahead of them. It was evident we were being helped from above, after having made the decision not to follow my career by moving to Omaha.

Moving never did feel like the right thing to do and it didn't work out the one time we had agreed to move there. So I had felt good about our decision to stay and begin our own business. But the last two of the seven years started to seem like an uphill battle, when it should actually have gotten easier.

Being in my mid fifties, this crisis felt much more daunting than any previously. I had started over numerous times, totally changing my career, without any doubt I would succeed. Having experienced and survived numerous illnesses/surgeries of my wife and family, building and losing a home, suffered severe depression, being successful and unsuccessful at business, surviving many threats to our marriage, and having grown from so many experiences in my life, I thought I was pretty much proven and experienced. Oh, how wrong I was.

Although fasting at times and continually praying, I was still frantic and terrified over losing the houses and the business. I was working in Sun Valley, Idaho one afternoon on a copper roof installation when I got the call. It reminded me of when Sara was in Pocatello and I was still in Coeur d Alene finishing construction on a house during the year from hell. Back then, she had called to tell me she had cancer. It seemed like the whole world stopped spinning that day. My perspectives were suddenly all put into place.

For months prior to receiving the current call, the critical status of my business and mortgage issues had left me unable to think clearly. I couldn't carry on a conversation with anyone without my mind totally checking out and not really listening to them. I couldn't force myself to be concerned with what they were saying. I really had to hold back tears when someone would ask how business was going.

I knew we had probably kept employees long after we should have, because I felt responsible for them and their families. We hadn't taken a pay check for the previous six months, just so we could pay them and some of our other depts. That put our personal life in jeopardy as well as our business. We had put all our profits back into the business over the past years to keep us from having debt if and when hard times may hit.

My emotional state seemed to be teetering on a ledge. There were so many nights that I could not sleep and would break out in a cold sweat, as my mind searched frantically for a solution I may have overlooked. Knowing my life was worth more through collected life insurance; I tried to block my failure of providing for my family from my mind. I would never consider taking my own life; but, I wished I could simply forget to keep breathing due to all that was happening in my mind.

As with the call years ago, my heart again sank as everything around me seemed to freeze in place. Sara began to tell me of a hole in her heart that the doctor had found after doing some tests. They told her it could be life threatening, as it may lead to a fatal stroke.

After completing our phone conversation I went up to my equipment trailer that was parked in a lot above the house. I poured out my heart to God. I walked outside but was still not able to return to where the crew was working. I walked up the secluded canyon on a dirt road. I continued to beg and plead with God. I feared I would not be able to go on without Sara. Each year I had become more and more dependent on her, she being my reason to live. Not sure if it was permissible to bargain with God, I found myself begging him to take everything I had, but to just leave Sara with me. In return I would praise him forever no matter what other things I had to suffer. All cried out and finding no words left to offer up, I closed my prayers. After I composed myself and hid my eyes behind sunglasses, I went back to where my crew was working.

I returned home later that week and we began to make preparations for surgery. Sara agreed to let me give her a blessing. Before surgery, a brain scan allowed them to determine she had already had two previous strokes. That was assurance we were doing the right thing. I also felt that maybe the previous symptoms that lead to the initial tests were a blessing.

Just before her surgery I had a peace come over me. The tears were gone. I knew that somehow everything would work out. And the greatest relief came as I had a confirmation within my heart that Sara would be alright.

That week I continued to feel relieved even though nothing had taken place yet. But I felt the calm I had prayed so hard for, in the midst of the current turbulence. I didn't fear losing everything. If I still had my family, I knew that would really be all I needed. My greatest fear had been that I would not be able to provide for them. But I suddenly knew I would be able to provide for them in some manner no matter what happened.

Weeks after Sara's surgery the youth leaders and the young men and young women from the Ward met at the church to begin a fast together. The Bishop spoke to them briefly about fasting, and then he offered a group prayer as we all knelt in a circle. The following afternoon they were all going to the temple to do baptisms for the dead and then would conclude the fast.

I didn't go to the temple with them but I did go to the group prayer and fasted with them. That fast was very special to me. After the group prayer a person came up to me and told me all the adult leaders were fasting for Sara and I. They were aware of our struggles and wanted me to know that they were praying for us. That gave me such added strength to face what was going on.

Days later as I pondered things, an interesting thing came to mind. I remembered how months before our financial problems peaked, I had sold our boat. We initially believed things were going to turn around. So since I selfishly felt I had given everything up for the past seven years, Sara agreed I should buy a motorcycle. I couldn't buy the bike however; because I couldn't get past an uneasy feeling in the pit of my stomach.

Instead I bought food storage and paid some bills. Then things got real bad and I was so glad I had listened to that little voice whispering in my ear.

After Sara's successful surgery we celebrated a great Thanksgiving with all our kids and my brother and his family. It was a continuation of a 20 year old tradition. That additionally helped to clarify that family is the most important thing in our lives. My eyes were opened to how blessed we were to live where the doctors and hospitals are some of the best in the country; which was important with Sara's condition.

Everyone kept telling me they were worried for me as I dealt with the pressure of the business, house, and then Sara. They were afraid I would cave under the pressure; being unaware of how much relief I had received from the pressure or burden through the fasting and praying of others and myself. I read from my journal about the year in Cour d Alene, when we went through that similar experience. I could see that after even the darkest times, things get better and a brighter day appears on the horizon.

I knew that God had always blessed me and would always bless me. I thought of the day when this trial is over and we won't have to live with temptation so great, the ugliness of sin around us, and the constant power struggle that creates greed for the things of this world. I longed to see Jesus and God the Father's face. But until then, I knew it was a blessing to live in marvelous times when we would watch things unfold that have been prophesied for years.

It seemed obvious to me that these were the times we have been warned of forever. I had studied them and been so interested in prophesied times that I almost looked forward to them. Not wanting to experience difficult times necessarily, but wanting to be part of whatever comes with the return of Christ. I always felt that knowing what was happening would take away all the sting of hard times. I can tell you now that it doesn't.

I realized I was watching people, so blindly, play roles that I had tried to picture in my mind for years; wondering how things prophesied could actually happen. It became evident that many people explain away what is happening due to wickedness, and ignore it or blame it on nature or chance. Some curse God for being so cruel or uncaring. Yet they fail to take the blame for their actions and refuse to admit that the warnings in scripture may be the cause of things happening around them. The words of prophets telling of our days are so precise and accurate in the scriptures. Yet so few will look at it and realize these are the times and situations told of. Blame for world economy collapses are directed toward various things. But the more man tries to stop all these thing, the faster it seems to fall. For years I could not figure out how things could really get bad everywhere simultaneously. But an example had just happened right before our eyes and at such an alarming rate; it was nearly unbelievable. Things improve slightly for a short time and all memories are then washed clean; rather than being thankful for the warning and preparing for future troubles.

With the calmness I felt after the youth fast, I knew all would be well with us. I could lose my house, my business, or anything else of temporal wealth in my life, but if I still had my wife and family all would be well. Again, I vowed to never curse God for what happened in my life; but instead praise him for what he had given me.

The last six months of Retro and the following six proved to be more trying than anything in my life even until now. I found myself being tested in ways I did not know existed. My successes and even my failures to that point had taught me who God was and who I was. Even my failures had taught me to believe in myself. I knew I could succeed at anything with God's help. My past had left me with a feeling that those who knew me probably felt I had integrity and was an honest person. That dark time strained all those feelings and beliefs. Even just before the final months of Retro I still believed I could be stripped of everything and still be fine and be strong. I found there were still a lot of things about me that had not been tested before. And even thought I thought I had been tested greater than a lot of people already, it seemed it was only a precursor to what I or we ended up having to experience.

After hitting the wall I realized I could not continue to live like that. I let the few remaining employees go and I shut down the business. A business grossing one million dollars in sells, with little remaining debt, was reduced to equipment being sold to pay outstanding tax debt. Our house was sold in a quick sale, with someone else being able to take advantage of that equity. The sale of the spec home covered the cost of construction, with someone else taking advantage of that equity.

Our retirement and personal money we put into the business was gone. Sara was suddenly unemployed because the company she was working for folded. After seven years of putting everything we had into the business, it all fell apart right before our eyes.

It wasn't the loss of the possessions I mourned, but the inability to provide for my family. A huge loss of receivables, left me no way to rectify my debts business relationships. For a time I felt helpless to lead my family through difficult times; which became my new nemesis.

After several months I had a friend that was looking to move to Utah. I helped her find a house that she eventually purchased. I then contracted to build out the full basement. Not able to move to Utah yet, we came to an agreement that we would stay in the house while I built it out. This helped us mutually as my rent came out of the work I was doing and it protected her house from vandalism, often experienced with vacant houses. This arrangement seemed too good to be true, and certainly not by chance.

I had no success in looking for employment during the months I built out the basement. My age and qualifications both seemed to be a disadvantage to me as I could not even get an interview. Then one day I had this idea I should call my previous employer and see if there was anything I could apply for. Amazingly enough, the Salt Lake Telecom Manager position was opened; which I had held ten years earlier. I applied and was given an interview. They called me at the end of the day and offered me the job. I was so thrilled but something inside would not let me fully celebrate. Two days later I received a call and they told me HR would not let them fill the position from outside the company.

Four months went by and I was all but done with the remodel and still no luck finding a job. I suddenly remembered seeing a technician opening on the company website, when I had applied for the manager position. I went to the computer but could not find any technician positions available. I called the General Director and asked him about that tech position. He indicated they had held interviews for that position that day and would hold the rest of them the next day. He told me, if I was in Roseville, Ca. at 8 am the following day, I could get an interview. It was already 2 pm so there was no way to get a flight. So I packed a suitcase and hit the highway.

I planned to get to my brother's house by about midnight. He lived about a half hour away from where the interviews were being held. But a severe winter storm made every effort to keep me from getting across the Sierra Mountains that night. I arrived the next morning with enough time to get a half hour nap and take a shower before going to the interview session.

The fifteen hour drive had the reverse effect it should have had. I prayed and pondered about all that had transpired during the past eight years. I remembered so many great times but relived so many troubled days and nights. During the hours of conversation with God I began to feel clarity I thought would never return. Technology from my previous telecom life bubbled to the surface, things I had not thought of or used for nearly a decade. Yet somehow it seemed so fresh. I stepped out of the car after arriving and felt renewed.

The session began with about 4 hours of testing. I probably tested better than I would have when I was instructing and managing the telecom training center years earlier. The fog was gone and answers seemed so easy to deliver. Then I had to wait as I was the last of 13 applicants to be interviewed. Panic would try to surface, but it was if a calming blanket seemed to smoother it. I sat outside and just enjoyed seeing the business operate around me. Ten minutes into the interview they gave me the job. The hiring panel consisted of a former peer and a person I had promoted prior to my departure. It was not stacked though, as they wanted another individual that had held the position previously. But that person did not pass the testing.

I thanked God nearly all the way home. Nothing had really transpired yet, but somehow so much had instantly been healed. I moved to California and began work as a telecom technician, a role I had began with over 20 years earlier. I could not have been happier. It was a single man territory so I had the opportunity to learn all the technology that had changed over the years. Most of my days were spend in the beautiful Feather River Canyon. Much of my territory consisted of remote and isolated microwave sites. Days were spent working alone in some of God's most beautiful creation. I can't even begin to describe the healing therapy that God provided me for a year and a half. I was then offered a promotion that enabled me to move back to Salt Lake

In just over two years of that youth fast, my world was transformed into something I could not have even dreamed of. If God would have given me a book and told me to write what I would want to happen on that day, I would not have even dared to ask for life to rebound so magnificently or quickly. I would question that it could logically be possible and would definitely have felt very greedy to ask for so much, in such a short amount of time. The promotion I received was to a Regional Manager, nearly what I was doing when I left the company. It was better than the original manager job I interviewed for and didn't receive.

Eight years after returning to the railroad I received wage increases and bonuses to place me at a level higher than I was when I left. My retirement was also reestablished, making me eligible for an incentivized early retirement program that was offered. Qualifying for the program by a few months, I decided to retire three years early. Having to work for nine years to break even, if not taking the incentive program, made the decision easy. Although I felt highly guilty to retire early, the math cleared my conscience. Those are things I would not have thought possible in the prior dark days.

I wish so badly I could get everyone together that participated in the youth fast. It would mean so much to me to be able to thank them. And what a testament it would be for them to hear of the success that transpired due to their sacrifice and efforts on our behalf.

The struggles and good times have given me much to ponder and write about over the years. My Patriarchal Blessing instructed me to write my family's history. I have tried to do that throughout the years. I believe that having access to your own previous experiences can provide many blessings. Hard times and joyful times forgotten are brought back to life when read. Occasionally when reading back through the years, you may begin to see a path that was so masterfully laid out for you. You may discover a path that provided choices, growth and learning; which you overlooked at the time it was happening. Those experiences you will hold so dear to your heart after leaving this life, when such opportunity to grow and prove yourself may no longer be available.

Recently after reading back through those trials I felt compelled to confess to my wife. Asking for her forgiveness, I told her much of what we went through was probably my fault. I had prayed that the Lord could take everything we had, but begged Him to please leave her with me. She laughingly asked me to not pray that way ever again.

Chapter 13

THE FINAL JUDGEMENT

My workday began with a flight from Salt Lake to Omaha. It was a dreary dark day with snow spitting from the violent looking sky. The bumpy ride down the runway through turbulent air did nothing to ease the tension in the cabin. Finally the wheels escaped the surface of the runway as the nose of the plane adjusted to a steep climb. The flashing of snow and clouds passing the window emphasized the speed of the plane. Moments later the engines were cut back slightly, the sensation of climbing diminished and the angle of ascent was quickly neutralized.

The air smoothed and I could almost feel a collective calm settle in. The dense darkness surrounding the plane seemed to flee as we gently rose above the clouds. All sensation of speed was immediately eliminated as the clouds were now a considerable distance below.

Looking out the window to my left, the dramatic change of scenery caused a feeling of reverence to drape me. The dark clouds replaced by an endless field of brilliant white; extended to where the vivid blue canopy began. A calming caused a long, slow exhale. It felt as though the Spirit had something to teach me. My mind marveled at the contrast experienced in such a short time. I had traveled from a darkened world that seemed to hurl as much ugliness as possible at me; to suddenly find myself motionless, viewing a scene of the great creation of

The Master. The brilliant contrasting blue and white seemed to enlighten me throughout the workday; feeling as if I had received a glimpse into heaven.

Arriving at my motel room in early evening, I was finally able to let my mind contemplate the feelings of the day. The beauty of the creation and the marvelous world our Father in Heaven has shared with us was my initial focus. Soon; however, my thoughts were turned to the great Day of Judgment and the contrasting experiences that may occur between people. Most people, I believe, hope for an experience as I had felt that morning; rising from a darkened world to find a reward of such peace and beauty. My mind was not able to explore that scene of beauty with any depth, as I was suddenly thinking of my childhood days in the public school system. Correlations seemed evident between the dreary beginning of the morning flight and the dreaded days of receiving my report cards. I couldn't seem to push to the point when the flight became beautiful. Instead my mind seemed to be stuck wading thought those years that I experienced much difficulty.

School was challenging for me, even from the first grade. Prior to the first grade, I was probably more excited to go to school than ninety percent of the preschoolers in America. However, even that level of excitement can be dashed to pieces by a negative experience; possibly determining how life is viewed for years to come.

My first grade teacher was a couple years from retirement and I would guess had not felt a single emotion for at least 20 years. By mid-year, I hated school and everything associated with it. For a couple years, I checked out of school early numerous times a month. A chronicle stomach ache, caused pain while just trying to breathe. Through my mother's extensive effort, she remained unable to link the forced shallow breathing to eating patterns or items eaten; also mystifying our family doctor. By the third grade I was put in a transition class. The transition class was composed of students that had been close to flunking the second grade. There were too many to hold back in the second grade, so they developed a transition class in hopes of getting the whole lot, ready for the fourth grade. We had a very caring and excellent teacher, who successfully passed all but a couple of the twenty students.

The class was made up of boys and girls that were obnoxious, unruly, non-motivated and largely from my first grade class (imagine that). The struggle to just achieve a passing grade continued throughout high school. I don't mean to imply I could barely pass due to my ability, because I know it was strictly due to my desire.

With about nine weeks left in my senior year, I received my first truancy. A group of us just couldn't resist the urge to spend one of those great spring days up a canyon four-wheeling. The boy's councilor called me into his office. He presented me with a form; which I was to take home and have my parents sign. I refused to do that, telling him I was going to Washington to live with my brother, planning to finish school there. The debate between the two of us continued, over whether or not I would finish school if I left so close to the end of the year. We then got to the root of why I would be willing to risk giving up so much, when the close of the year was so near. I could not take that notice home, for my mother to sign, no matter what the cost. It wasn't because I feared the discipline I might receive. The thing I could not bear was to see the disappointment and hurt on my mother's face one more time, over some stupid thing I had done. After the counselor adamantly told me he knew I would not finish school if I moved, he said he would let me forge my parent's signature if I promised to stay in school and finish. I could not pass up a deal like that.

The counselor's actions that day had one of the greatest impacts on me that I had experienced in all 12 years of schooling. There had been great teachers and coaches that had motivated and helped me at various times. My high school wrestling coach taught me a lot about desire and motivation, whose lessons have helped me to this day. But the action taken by that counselor prevented my education from ending with the same tone it had begun with.

I know I am not the only person who has eagerly awaited a report card to be posted. Some people waited with great expectations of joy and others of us waited with hopes of a gift of charity. But once the card hit our doorstep, our work was complete and we could see the final results of our actions and efforts. We could be proud and feel great resolve or we could feel that useless feeling of wishing there was some way to change the outcome we had received. We may say, "If only we had tried a little harder, having spent just a few more evenings studying instead of doing those things that provided very temporary gratification". In my case, I was usually left to live with grades that were to stand for the rest of time; a grade that I knew was far less than I could have achieved. I then had to accept the outcome and try to overcome its lasting brand, by means of harder work than originally would have been necessary. There were so many people in my classes that received higher grades than I did. However, I knew I actually had more potential than they did, but opted not to use it.

With that walk down memory lane, the mood within my room was rather dark and somber. My heart was heavy and all those years of anxiety and bad memories had deflated the cloud I had walked on throughout the day. Now it seemed my mind was ready to move on, as my thoughts were suddenly focused on my final judgment. Intense regret and disappointment fell upon me, as I began to feel the weight of my sins heavy upon my back. It was as if my time was up and the deeds and actions of my life were now culminated, with no way offered for further repentance. The feeling of a bad report card was only a pittance of the worthlessness and sorrow that began pushing me to my knees. As tears filled my eyes, I began pleading with my Father in Heaven for His forgiveness and mercy. I was not aware if my eyes were open or not, but suddenly an image momentarily flashed before me. It was as if a camera shutter opened for a moment and then quickly closed. My perspective was as if I was kneeling on the floor. Directly in front of me, a personage was stepping from the second step of a slightly raised stage, onto the floor where I knelt. He was dressed in a flowing white robe. There were a number of men standing upon the stage to each side; however, their images were somewhat muted, taking no focus from the main individual stepping toward me.

The image was gone as quickly as it came. However, the momentary flash, while being taught by the Spirit, caused the gloom to flea and an immense joy filled my heart. In a single moment of time, I received feelings as if having experienced my entire judgment session. The emotions spanned from nervously entering the room, to then be individually judged by that Great Bar of Justice, and then hear the final words of my Savior. I wrote the following after an emotional experience; which was felt, not seen.

****

Slowly I walked to the Judgment Hall, the weight so heavy upon my back. It seemed futile to delay stepping through the doorway to face the council that would judge my life; an assembly of men so great they could see into my very heart and mind. I was not sure I could bear the look on my dear Savior's face as He looked into my heart and saw the darkness that resided there. I stood at the door, knob in hand, thinking of all the times during my mortal life when even a small amount of effort could have reaped benefits. I recalled the small acts of kindness I had casually passed by; which would have cost so little at the time; but would now have eternal benefits.

Breathing deeply, I tried to stop the tears that began flowing freely. Many wonderful souls came to mind that I knew had certainly earned a place where they would find happiness and joy.

A smile actually formed on my lips as I realized, regardless of all the levels of inequality that existed on Earth, a person who had lived with the *least* amount of temporal possessions now had the opportunity to live in a palace far better than anything that had ever been available to the inhabitants of Earth. For some unexplainable reason, I remembered the people I had known on Earth who thought the only thing that mattered was their physical appearance, and how surprised they had been when they left Earth and found that their inner qualities were more visible and adored than their physical characteristics.

I turned the knob and pushed the door open. How I wished I could have had my wife by my side to help him shine. I had always felt invisible when she was not with me. But now I was to be judged strictly on my own merit.

As Christ entered the room, I felt as if I were suddenly stripped naked. Not of clothing, but of pride. Every weakness and character flaw I had let develop within me was totally exposed. I could not raise my eyes from the floor, as every moment of my life began to flash before me. It was not a quick momentary flash of a few events. Instead, it was every moment and event since my birth. The secrets I had hidden from everyone were now exposed to sacred, righteous entities, which now stood directly in front of me. In some miraculous way, the knowledge that I could not achieve eternal exaltation through my own efforts alone came to mind. I prayed fervently that Jesus Christ would find the decisions I had made on Earth, qualified me to receive the mercy offered through His Atonement.

The review of my life continued. As I viewed a misdealing with a partner, or a lie I thought I had gotten away with, the images stopped. The individual I had wronged entered the room. I had to confess what I had done, how I had wronged them, and what I gained by my misdeed, all while looking directly into that person's eyes, and then I had to ask for their forgiveness. If no one on Earth witnessed a sin, the Book of Life was opened and a member of the Judgment Counsel read what those on the other side of the veil had witnessed and recorded. Their account was identical to the one my own memory provided my eyes. Once I had confessed my sin, the moments of my life again continued forward from that point.

Throughout my judgment, I found it extremely difficult to continue standing in the presence of my Great Father, Jesus Christ and those on the panel. I looked at the scars still visible on my Savior's hands and feet, and felt total and complete sorrow that my sins had added to the suffering the Savior had been forced to endure. I was grateful that the terrible things I had previously repented of were now absent from the activities I saw replayed from my life. I was grateful that each sin I had repented of increased the possibility that I might spend eternity with my wife. I wished I had the ability to rewind the hands of time, live a moment of weakness over again and make the right decision.

The images of my life were finally completed. The witnesses had all come forward, allowing me to admit my guilt. Now I was alone standing before the judges. I forced myself to slowly raise my eyes from the floor. The nervousness that had nearly consumed me when I first entered the room was gone. For the first time I actually looked around. All of God's chosen were now sitting in a semi-circle in front of me on beautiful white thrones. Christ sat in the middle upon His throne. The walls were a beautiful weave of white material different from any fabric I had known before. The floor was one continuous piece of white marble stretching from wall to wall.

The entire room appeared luminescent. Although no direct source of light could be detected, the room glowed with brilliance. The light was so pure and warming that it felt as if it embraced and soothed me. The left and right ends of the room appeared to have no visible walls. The room itself seemed to be floating between the two realms – the one on the right and the one on the left. The light visible from the left side of the room reminded me of a dreary heavily overcast day. Streaming into the room from the right was golden light that carried sweet fragrances and sounds that reminded me of my very favorite places on earth.

The difference between the two areas, right and left, was immense. It was much greater than the difference between being below the clouds on a dark, dreary, rainy day, and being above them where the sun warmed everything it touched and caused the clouds to glow brightly against the deep blue sky.

Suddenly I was pulled back to the reality of what was taking place as Christ called me by name. In a very gentle, understanding, and caring voice He asked, "Viewing all that you have said and done throughout your life, knowing the talents and blessings you were given, did you help to benefit or destroy your fellow man and all my creation? Your decision will determine if you pass to your right or left."

The decision had fallen upon my shoulders; the weight drove me to the floor. As I knelt there, hands and knees pressed against the marble, every fiber of my being wanted to run through the entry to the right, but I knew what I deserved. The regret of every mistake and sin I had made during my life on Earth seemed magnified a thousand times, totally overwhelming me. I tried to confess that I knew I had been foolish and could have done so much better, but the words would not come. I sobbed uncontrollably, knowing that it all ended at that moment, and I would never have another chance to change anything I had done during my test on the Earth.

Suddenly, I felt myself being helped to my feet. Christ embraced me and I let my sorrow flow freely. I could feel warm energy radiating from my Savior and spreading through every cell in my own body. I wanted to stay right there and never have to face the moment that loomed ahead.

Christ slowly helped me move toward the end of the room and then said, "Our Father said it would be very difficult and we would lose many of those dear to us. You fell often, but you struggled until you got back up. Although you wandered from side to side, you always walked in my direction. You have a long time to work on your weaknesses. But without going to Earth, you would not have gained understanding and compassion for your fellow man."

I opened my eyes and looked at the Savior, not able to see Him clearly because of the tears that filled my eyes. I tried to stand on my own and forced myself to turn and look at the portal I would now be required to step through.

"Well done, my son," the Savior said softly.

I personally believe that it will be a struggle to earn the right to dwell with our Father in Heaven in His kingdom. But I have hope that it is obtainable. Through a lot of improvement day after day, and pleading for the gift of Jesus Christ's atonement, I hope I will be ushered through the gates to God's kingdom.

There are so many things I have sought answers to. In each; if I studied, pondered, and prayed, the tiny seed of faith has been replaced with a solid and cherished knowledge.

I wish so badly that I could give you the feeling of certainty that my soul has, in regard to the things I have shared. The Spirit has burned these answers upon my heart. I pray that you may be, so blessed, in seeking your answers through prayer.

OTHER BOOKS BY THE AUTHOR

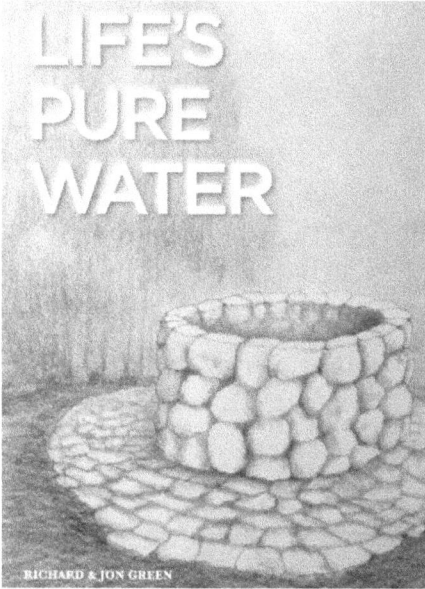

A collection of poems and thoughts; written by brothers Richard and Jon Green. Realizing they had each unknowingly been writing similar themed material for decades, they decided to combine their work that focuses on the Savior, family, and life experiences.

LIFE'S PURE WATER
Available on Amazon
ISBN 9780991516322

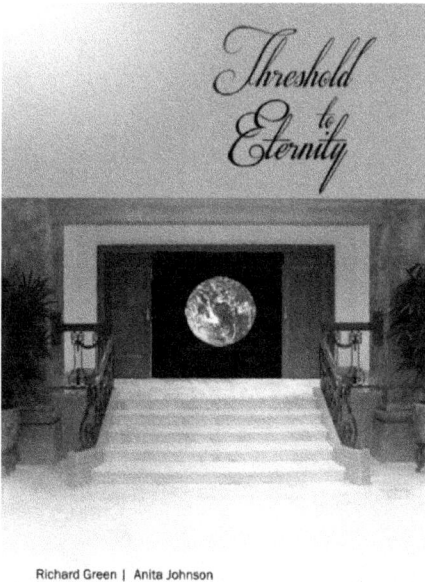

Richard and his sister Anita combined efforts to write a thought provoking fictional novel, based on the plan of salvation. Follow a small group of friends as their time spans from life on a newly created earth, to a final judgment and the end of life as we know it.

THRESHOLD to ETERNITY
Available on Amazon
ISBN 9780991516360

www.ingramcontent.com/pod-product-compliance
Lightning Source LLC
LaVergne TN
LVHW021402080426
835508LV00020B/2415